THE MAIN STREET DICTIONARY OF DOLL MARKS

THE MAIN STREET DICTIONARY OF DOLL MARKS

by Jean Bach

Vicki Brooks, General Editor
Marks rendered by Frank Mahood
with the assistance of
Lisa Magaz and John Fox

THE MAIN STREET PRESS • PITTSTOWN, NEW JERSEY

First edition 1985

All rights reserved

Copyright © 1985 by The Main Street Press

Published by
The Main Street Press
William Case House
Pittstown, New Jersey 08867

Published simultaneously in Canada by
Methuen Publications
2330 Midland Avenue
Agincourt, Ontario M1S 1P7

Printed in the United States of America

Jacket and text design by Frank Mahood

Library of Congress Cataloging in Publication Data

Bach, Jean.
   The Main Street dictionary of doll marks.

   Bibliography: p.
   Includes indexes.
   1. Dolls—trademarks. 1. Title.
NK4893.3.B33 1985   688.7′221′0275   85-24048
ISBN 0-915590-57-3

CONTENTS

INTRODUCTION

DOLL collectors are intrepid, indefatigable hunters, tireless in their search for perfect additions to their collections, and matchless in their enthusiasm when they discover the ideal doll. Many of them, it is true, are more concerned with the look of the doll, its type, and its condition than with its maker. That notwithstanding, there is no doubt that knowing the manufacturer, country of origin, and approximate age of the doll adds greatly to its value and to the satisfaction of owning it. Discovering this pertinent information about a newly acquired doll is part of the fun of the chase. And while materials, features, style of painting, and other obvious characteristics can help in identifying the doll, its mark or marks provide corroboration and often positive identification.

There are millions of dolls in thousands of collections throughout the world, and doll collecting continues to rise in popularity (exceeded only, according to a recent magazine article, by stamp collecting). It therefore follows that the number of available collectible dolls made from about 1840 to 1940, the century upon which this book focuses, is dwindling, and that there is a ready market to be tapped by the unscrupulous, who seek to foist cheap reproductions upon the unwary collector. Learning to identify dolls by their marks is basic to avoiding such pitfalls.

Long before dolls became popular toys for children and before they were mass-produced to make them affordable, porcelain manufacturers were marking their products to signify their origin and quality. As the market for dolls increased, many such factories turned to manufacturing dolls (or dolls' heads) and marked these new products, as well. Prior to 1891, however, there were no regulations regarding such identification—trademarks-were thus a matter of choice, left to the discretion of the individual manufacturer. Many dolls, of course, were also made of materials other than bisque or porcelain—leather, papier mâché, and cloth among them—materials not so easily marked in a permanent way. Therefore, a large percentage of dolls made prior to the 1890s were not marked at all. In 1891, a United States trade law required all imports to be marked to indicate country of origin. By then the great majority of dolls manufactured in Europe, Britain, and Asia was destined for America, making identification of post-1891 dolls easier for today's collectors. The law was subject to wide interpretation, however. Sometimes packing materials, rather than the dolls themselves, were marked; or the identification might be in the form of a paper label or tag affixed to the doll (a form of "mark" easily subjected to wear or loss over the years).

One of the challenges of doll identification is that few generalities can be made about the appearance of marks, the way in which they are applied, or their location. As you will see when you peruse this book, marks come in all shapes and types, from simple initials, to numbers, to names and phrases, to figures and symbols, or combinations of all of them. Marks can appear on the back of the head (often obscured by a wig), on the shoulder plate, on the chest or back, or even on the soles of the feet. They can be incised into the material, raised, stamped, or attached in the form of a label, sticker, or decal. Often a doll will contain several quite disparate marks because few manufacturers made both the head and the body, finding it more efficient to order one or the other from another maker. Many firms, such as Simon & Halbig, Armand Marseille, and Hertel, Schwab, concentrated on supplying heads for other companies; in these cases, you'll often find a combination of the porcelain factory's mark and that of the company for which the head was made incised on the same doll.

All of this may sound quite complicated to the new collector, but don't despair. This book is arranged to help you find the marks you're seeking with a minimum of difficulty. The first section contains an alphabetical listing of manufacturers and distributors; typical marks are shown within these listings, and lists of trade names are given when applicable. (Designers are included in this section when their own marks appeared on the dolls they created.) In addition, there are six indexes at the back of the book. Regardless of the basic composition of the mark you are trying to identify, you'll want to begin with these indexes. There is an alphabetical index of initials and letters, one of names and phrases, and one of symbols. In addition, there is a numeric index of mold numbers and one of dates found on marks. And finally, there is an index of the designers who created some of the most appealing dolls, but who were in no way responsible for their manufacture. (We have *not* included marks that remain unidentified, since the basic purpose of this book is to help collectors positively identify their dolls.)

Bear in mind that it would be impossible to include in this one volume each and every mark used by each and every American, British, European, or Asian manufacturer from 1840 to 1940. Marks that are *representative* of the manufacturer have therefore been selected for inclusion, as well as other information (such as known mold numbers, variations in initials and names, and materials used) vital to the identification of antique dolls.

The wise collector knows how important it is to recognize the difference

D.R.G.M.
357 529

between a mold number and a size or patent number. A patent number is generally easy to spot. Most frequently, as in the Louis Lindner patent number illustrated, the multidigit number is preceded by the initials *D.R.G.M.* (i.e., *Deutsches Reichsgebrauchsmuster* or German design patent). The sample Armand Marseille mark illustrated here shows both a mold number and the size of the doll, in addition to the company's identification. As in this case, size numbers are usually single- or two-digit numbers, often incorporating fractions and/or letters. (Size and patent numbers are *not* included in the numerical index at the back of the book.)

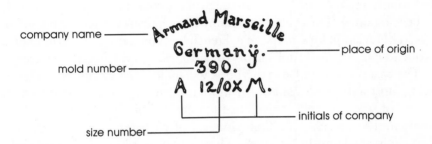

company name ——— Armand Marseille
Germany. ——— place of origin
mold number ——— 390.
A 12/0x M.
——— initials of company
size number ———

While a company may have introduced a specific mold number in a given year, often the mold was used for a number of years thereafter; it is therefore difficult to date a doll precisely using just its mold number. The same rule applies to trade names: we have listed the date when a named doll was first introduced, but that should not be construed as its date of manufacture. In fact, the dates are approximate, since in many cases the same doll was registered in several countries, not necessarily all in the same year.

One of the problems for those of us who aren't multilingual is that many marks are couched in the language of the country of origin, though most dolls intended for the American market were marked in English. Some of the most prevalent words, phrases, and initials you'll find in French are:

Breveté (or **Bté.**)—patented
Déposé (or **Dep.**)—registered
Fabrication française—French-made
Jouet—toy
Marque déposée—registered mark
Medaille d'or—gold medal-winner

Poupée—doll

SGDG (i.e., *sans garantie du governement*)—without government warranty

Some of the German words you're likely to find are:

Deponiert (or dep.)—registered
DRGM (i.e., *Deutsches Reichsgebrauchsmuster*)—registered design
DRP (i.e., *Deutsches Reichspatent*)—patent
Fabrik-marke—trademark
Gesetzlich geschützt (or Ges. gesch.)—patent rights registered
GM (i.e., *Geschmacksmuster*)—design patent
Holzmasse — wooden composition
Schutz marke — trademark
Wimpern — eyelashes

In listing company names, the language of the country of origin has usually been retained. Thus you'll find many French firms whose names end in *Cie*. (abbreviation for *Compagnie*, French for "company"). A German firm is often a *Puppenfabrik* (doll factory) or a *Porzellanfabrik* (porcelain factory).

The basic facts included in this book will undoubtedly help you in identifying most antique dolls; but for more information, you'll want to turn to one of several excellent reference sources. Scholarly interest in dolls is comparatively recent; the first pioneers of such research were Evelyn, Elizabeth, and Dorothy Coleman, whose *Collector's Encyclopedia of Dolls* (1968) remains a classic in the field, especially with reference to French and American dolls. As great as the Colemans' contributions are, however, much of their information on German dolls has been eclipsed by the recent publication of Jürgen and Marianne Cieslik's *German Doll Encyclopedia* (1985). The Ciesliks' scholarship is unparalleled and collectors will be in their debt for many years to come. I am happy to acknowledge at least part of that debt here, since the present book would have been the poorer without reference to their scholarly revelations.

As Ecclesiastes declares, "to the making of books there is no end." And this book is hardly an exception. A second edition will undoubtedly include many marks that, posing mysteries today, will be identified by collectors tomorrow. In the meantime, I am happy to acknowledge the enthusiastic support and assistance of my editors, Vicki Brooks and Martin Greif, and of the artists whose skill enabled the many marks in this book to be rendered with such precision: John Fox, Lisa Magaz, and Frank Mahood.

A

A la Poupée de Nuremberg
Paris

Wooden and kid-bodied lady dolls sold by this shop in the late 1860s carried a label similar to the one illustrated here.

Abraham & Straus
Brooklyn, New York

Established in 1903, this American retailer is still in business today. The company distributed a wide variety of dolls. One trademark, **Baby Violet**, was registered by the firm in 1906.

Emma E. Adams
Oswego, New York

Emma Adams (and her sister, Marietta) began creating rag dolls filled with cotton and sawdust in 1891. The dolls, distributed by Marshall Field, varied in size and type—from babies to boys and girls. Each was stamped as indicated here. Hair and features were hand-painted. Upon Emma Adams' death (after 1900), the stamp was revised to include Marietta's married name, Ruttan.

COLUMBIAN DOLL
EMMA E. ADAMS
OSWEGO
N.Y.

THE COLUMBIAN DOLL
MANUFACTURED BY
MARIETTA ADAMS RUTTAN
OSWEGO, N.Y.

Älteste Volkstedter Porzellan-fabrik
(see Rudolph Heinz & Co.)

Aich, Menzel & Co.
Aich, Bohemia

Founded in 1848, this porcelain firm changed hands several times, under the direction of M.J. Möhling in 1870, A.C. Anger in 1893, and Ludwig Engel in 1910. It gained the Aich, Menzel name in 1918, at which time it began making dolls' heads.

1904-13
A̶e̶.M
Made in Austria

Frederic Aldis
London

As his mark implies, Aldis sold dolls (both domestic and imported). Established in 1878, his firm also manufactured dolls and dolls' bodies. He is known to have used Pierotti wax heads for some of his creations.

Alexander Doll Co.
New York City

The dolls of Beatrice Alexander Behrman and the Alexander Doll Company are so popular with modern collectors that entire books have been written about them. The reasons for this popularity are twofold:

1

they are comparatively well made by American standards and many of them display an incisive feeling for subject matter that is popular at a given moment. Madame Alexander has had a knack, at least since the 1930s, for making portrait dolls of the very people and literary characters who seem to personify an age: the **Dionne Quintuplets, Jane Withers, Sonja Henie,** and **Scarlett O'Hara** among them. Madame Alexander's first rag dolls date from the 1920s and include such endearing favorites as **Meg, Jo, Beth,** and **Amy** from *Little Women,* **Alice in Wonderland,** and many characters from the novels of Dickens.

The problem for the collector is not in locating these dolls, but in identifying them beyond any doubt: many of the Madame Alexander dolls are not marked permanently, but were issued with only wrist tabs and/or cloth labels attached to their clothing. A few, such as **Princess Elizabeth,** can be identified by the cross within a circle which appears on the head; others were stamped **Alexander** or **Mme Alexander** on the head or torso. **Hansel** and **Gretel, Rip van Winkle,** and other marionettes designed by Tony Sarg for Alexander were marked **Tony Sarg** on the heads. Among the many character dolls issued by the firm from the 1920s to the early '40s were:

Agnes (1934)
Amy (1923)
Beth (1923)
David Copperfield (1924)
Dionne Quintuplets (1935)
Dopey (1938)
Kate Greenaway (1938)
Hansel and **Gretel** (1934)
Sonja Henie (1939)
Jo (1923)
Little Colonel (1935—see mark)
Little Emily (1924)
Little Nell (1924)
Little Shaver (1934)
Lollie the 'Lov-le-Tex' Rubber Doll (1941)
McGuffey Ana (1937)
Meg (1923)
Scarlett O'Hara (1940)
Princess Elizabeth (1937)
Red Cross Nurse (1917)

Rip van Winkle (1934)
The Three Little Pigs (1933)
Tiny Tim (1924)
Oliver Twist (1924)
Jeannie Walker (1941)
Wendy-Ann (c. 1936)
Jane Withers (1937)

LITTLE COLONEL

Henri Alexandre
Paris

The short-lived Alexandre firm was named for the designer of the **Bébé Phénix** dolls, whose several dozen models were produced first by Alexandre (1889), then several years later by a firm called Tourrel, which merged with Jules Steiner in 1895.

Alt, Beck & Gottschalck
Nauendorf, Germany

Established in 1854 (as Porzellanfabrik von Alt), this porcelain factory is known to have made a variety of bisque heads, as well as all-bisque dolls. It was one of the German companies tapped by George Borgfeldt to supply heads for Grace Storey Putnam's astoundingly successful Bye-Lo in the 1920s, though it manufactured appealing character dolls of its own as well. The company's distinctive mark appears on Borgfeldt's Bonnie Babe as well as on dolls of its own manufacture, among them a line of nanking dolls it advertised in the early years of the 20th century. Bisque versions of some of American designer Jeanne Orsini's dolls were made by Alt, Beck & Gottschalck (see the Orsini entry for mark). The **Albego** mark is found only on dolls manufactured between 1930 and 1940.

Alt, Beck & Gottschalck mold numbers include: 128, 129, 138, 222, 639, 696, 698, 772, 784, 866, 867, 868, 869, 870, 880, 890, 894, 974, 979, 1000, 1008, 1020,

1024, 1026, 1028, 1044, 1046, 1056, 1062, 1064, 1086, 1092, 1121, 1123, 1142, 1152, 1153, 1170, 1171, 1172, 1173, 1174, 1175, 1176, 1177, 1210, 1222, 1226, 1234, 1235, 1236, 1237, 1250, 1254, 1260, 1261, 1268, 1269, 1270, 1271, 1279, 1288, 1290, 1291, 1321, 1322, 1326, 1342, 1346, 1352, 1353, 1357, 1358, 1360, 1361, 1362, 1366, 1367, 1368, 1373, 1376, 1402, and 1432.

ABG

1362

Made in Germany

3

A.B.&G.

1322/1

Deponiert

25

13 ABG 57

ABG

ABG

Germany

1360

19/0

1361

40

Made in Germany

ALBEGO

10

Made in Germany

Althof, Bergmann & Co.

New York City

Established in 1848, the firm of Althof,

Bergmann was perhaps best known as a successful toy importer, whose business mushroomed as the century wore on until, by the early 1880s, it was known as one of the largest toy jobbers in the country. Besides purchasing a great deal of its stock from France, Germany, Great Britain, and China, the jobber made its own line of mechanical dolls, which were applauded for their life-like movement. The company registered its trademark, **A.B.C.**, in 1881.

Louis Amberg & Son

Cincinnati and New York City

Founded in 1878 as a doll importer and jobber, Louis Amberg & Son began to manufacture its own composition dolls after 1903, while continuing to purchase many of its dolls from other American and European makers. The company's line of dolls, especially during the second decade of the 20th century, was enormous. With the outbreak of World War I (1914), Amberg inaugurated two advertising slogans—**American Dolls for Americans**, and **The American Standard**—both of which it used extensively while supplies from Europe were curtailed. Among the many trade names used on Amberg dolls were:

Amberg's Walking Doll (1919)
Ambisc (1915)
Amkid (1918)
Anniversary Baby (1924)
Baby Beautiful Dolls (1910)
Baby Boy, Model Number 1 (1911)
Baby Bright Eyes (1911)
Baby Glee (1915)
Baby Peggy (Baby Peggy The Nation's Darling) (1923)
Baby Tufums (see mark)
Baseball Boy (1913)
Beach Boy, Beach Girl (1915)
Bobby (1910)
Bobby Blake (1911)
Boy with Cap, Model No. 12 (1911)
Bright Eyes (1912)
Brother, Model No. 2 (1911)
Buster Boy (1911)
Charlie Chaplin (1915—see mark)
Clownie (1911)
College Kids (1912)
Cry Baby Bunting (1911)

Curly Locks (1911)
Daffydils (1912)
Dickie (1911)
Dixie Mascot (1911)
Dolly Drake (1911)
Dolly (1910)
Dorothy Dainty (1911—see mark dated 1911)
Dorothy Deer (1912)
Dutch Boy, Dutch Girl (1911)
The Educational Doll (1916)
The Faun (1912)
Fine Baby (1917)
First Steps (1916)
Florodora Sextet (1912)
Freshie (1921)
Girl with the Curl (1912)
Goody Goody (1915)
Hail Columbia (1913)
Harem Skirt Doll (1911)
Head of Baby (1921)
Head of Little Girl (nd)
Hiawatha (1911)
Honey Boy (1911)
I Walk-I Talk-I Sleep (1903)
Jack Tar (1914)
Jim Dandy (1914)
John Bunny Doll (1914)
Johnny Jones (1912)
Koaster Kid (1913)
Laughing Boy (1911)
Laughing Marietta (1912)
Little Bo-Peep (1912)
Little Boy Blue (1911)
Little Brother (1911)
Little Cherub (1915)
Little Fairy (1911)
Little Lord Fauntleroy (1911)
Little Red Riding Hood (1911)
Little Sister (1911)
Little Stranger (1912)
Little Sweetheart (1913)
Lucky Bill (1909)
Mama I'm Awake Baby (1919)
Marie Doll (1911)
Mibs (1921—see mark dated 1921)
Middy Boy, Middy Girl (1912)
Mildred Mine (Mildred) (1911)
Minnehaha (1911)
Miss Broadway (1912)
Miss Simplicity (1912)
My Best Friend (1911)
Nature Children (1921)

New Born [Nuborn] Babe (1914—see mark dated 1914)
Nibsie (1924)
Oliver Twist (1914)
Oo-Gug-Luk (1915)
Papa-Mama Doll (1903)
Patty-Cake (1925)
Peg O'My Heart (1914)
Pollyanna, The Glad Doll (1916)
Pouting Tots (1914)
Pudgie (1915)
Rainbow Dolls (1915)
Rosebud (1910)
Sassy Sue (1911)
School Boy, School Girl (1911)
School Boy with Cap (1911)
Sis Hopkins (1911—see mark)
Sister, Model No. 4 (1911)
Skookum, The Bully Kiddo (1916)
Soldier Boy (1914)
Span (1911)
Spearmint Kiddo (1912)
Spic (1911)
Sunny Jim (1909)
Sunny Orange Blossom (1924)
Swat Mulligan (1911)
Sweetheart (1915)
Tango Tots (1914)
Tiny Tads (1912)
Tiny Tots (1913)
Truest-to-Life (1913)
Twilite Baby (1915)
Vanta Baby (c. 1920s—see mark)
Victory Doll (1917—see mark)
Whistling Willie (1914)
The Wonder Baby (1913)
The World Standard (1918) [an advertising slogan found on heads]
Yankee Doodle (1912)

Baby Tufums
LA⋆S
107
Germany

CHARLIE CHAPLIN DOLL
WORLD'S GREATEST COMEDIAN
MADE EXCLUSIVELY BY LOUIS AMBERG & SON, N.Y.
by SPECIAL ARRANGEMENT WITH ESSANAY FILM CO.

L.A.S. ©
414
1911

LA&S 1921 ©
Germany

©L.A.& S. 1914
#G 45520
Germany #4

S¹²HºPK¹Nˢ

Vanta Baby
LA&S. 3/0 D.R.G.M.
Germany

ᴬMBERG'ˢ
VICTORY
ᴰOLL

LA&S
RA 241 5/0
GERMANY

GERMANY
A-R
LA&S 886.2

LA&S
RA 247/5/0
Germany

GERMANY
A·R
LA&S 886.2

American Bisque Doll Co.
Newark, New Jersey

American Bisque Doll Co.
Chicago

These two doll manufacturers were established in the same year (1919). It is not known for certain which used the mark il- lustrated here, though the New Jersey firm's trademark was thought to have included a rose with the words **American Beauty Doll** inscribed upon it. The eastern company was also the manufacturer of a doll which it called **Romper Boy** (1920).

American Character Doll Co.
New York City

The **Petite** trademark illustrated here was used on a line of composition character babies manufactured by American Character Doll Co. beginning in the early 1920s. Among the names given to dolls in the line were **Teenie Weenie** and **Walkie, Talkie, Sleepie**. Other infant and baby dolls (also composition) manufactured during the same period were **Baby's Pal**, **Baby's Joy**, and **Baby's Playmate**. The **Aceedeecee Doll** (1920) was the appellation given to the firm's wood-fiber composition dolls. A distinctive horseshoe was part of the trademark registered for new additions to the Petite line, including **Sally** (1930), **Sally Joy** (1931), and **Toodles** (1931).

The American Doll
New York City

Mary Haskell Lakopolanska registered this company trademark for dolls in 1939.

American Made Toy Co.
Brooklyn and New York City

Owned by Louis I. Bloom, this maker of stuffed dolls registered its trademark in 1929.

American Stuffed Novelty Co.
New York City

The Life Like Line of dolls made by American Stuffed Novelty Co. beginning in 1924 was distributed by Edwin A. Besser, Borgfeldt, and Louis Wolf & Co. The dolls were stuffed with cotton, their features painted by hand. Some of the trade names used for dolls in the line (beginning in 1925) were The Co-Ed Flapper, Flapper, King's Jester, Pierrot and Pierrette, and Trilby.

Anchor Toy Corp.
New York City

Founded in 1924, this American toy importer dealt primarily with German and French doll manufacturers. Its distinctive anchor trademark, therefore, is of little help in determining a doll's country (or company) of origin.

Félix Arena
Paris

Mignon was registered as a trademark by Félix Arena in 1918. It is probably safe to assume that many of Arena's dolls' heads were manufactured for him in Germany.

MIGNON

Max Oscar Arnold
Neustadt, Germany

Founded in 1878, the firm of Max Oscar Arnold was first noted for its mechanical dolls. As late as the first decade of the 20th century, Arnold was granted patents for a line of talking dolls, one of which was marked Arnola or Arnoldia, along with the number 54/14. The maker of the head has not been positively identified. Arnold's bisque heads, marked with the firm's initials within an eight-pointed star, date from the early 1920s; most were thought to have been manufactured for Welsch & Co. in Sonneberg.

SCHUTZ-MARKS.

Arnold Print Works
North Adams, Massachusetts

This dress goods manufacturer, founded in 1876, became one of the largest suppliers of printed fabrics in America. It also was known as a manufacturer of popular printed doll patterns which were to be cut out, sewn, and stuffed to create a number of whimsical, cuddly figures. The full-color patterns were printed on white cotton; the firm's mark was included on the cloth, though not within the pattern itself. Designs patented by Celia M. Smith and her sister-in-law, Charity Smith, were executed on the cloth, as were the **Brownies** of Palmer Cox, (1892) which became so popular that it is thought Kodak's Brownie camera was named after them. (Cox's copyright appeared on the sole of one foot.) Some of Celia Smith's creations, first produced around 1893, included **Columbia Sailor Boy, Little Red Riding Hood, Our Soldier Boys, Pickaninny, Pitti-Sing,** and **Topsy.** The dolls were distributed by Selchow & Righter.

Copyrighted. 1892
by PALMER COX

Arranbee Doll Co.
New York City

An importer of doll parts (which it assembled) and of dolls, Arranbee was established in 1922. By far its most celebrated offering was **My Dream Baby** (1924—also known simply as **Dream Baby**), whose bisque head was made by Armand Marseille in direct competition with Grace Storey Putnam's celebrated Bye-Lo. In addition, Arranbee registered a number of trade names, among them **Cherrie Historical Portrait Dolls** (1938), **Kurly Head** (1930), **Little Angel** (1940), and **Nancy** (1930).

Art Fabric Mills
New York City

Founded somewhat later (1899) than its major competitor, Arnold Print Works, this fabric manufacturer produced a number of colorful printed patterns for rag dolls. The company name was generally printed on the sole of one foot, the word "pat" and a date (signifying the date of patent, not of manufacture) on the other. **Life Size Dolls,** the most famous of Art Fabric's designs, were patented on February 13, 1900. Trade names of some of the other dolls include:

Baby (1907)
Billy (1907)
Bridget (1907)
Diana (1907)
Dolly Dimple (1909)
Foxy Grandpa (1905)
Newly Wed Kid (1907)
Tiny Tim (1909)
Topsy (1900)
Uncle (1907)

PAT. FEB. 13, 1900

The Art Metal Works
Newark, New Jersey

Known chiefly for a mama doll called **I Talk** (1914), The Art Metal Works was established in 1914, and in 1924 joined with other companies to found a company named Voices, Inc. Other metal dolls manufactured by the original firm included the **Treat 'Em Rough Kiddie** (1919), made of stamped brass with enameled, molded features.

Au Nain Bleu
Paris

In the latter half of the 19th century, Au Nain Bleu sold both French and German bisque-headed dolls, generally marked as indicated here. The shop was known to have distributed S.F.B.J. dolls, marked **Unis France,** in the early 1920s. It is not known

whether the "E. Chauviere" on the mark bears any relation to a company called Chauviere, which was known to have been in the doll business in Paris from 1848 until close to the end of the century.

Au Paradis des Enfants
Paris

A large toy and doll retailer founded in 1873, Au Paradis des Enfants sold both German and French doll manufacturer's products. The firm is known to have used both of the marks illustrated here.

Au Perroquet Cie.
Paris

Registered the trademark **La Négresse Blonde** for dolls, 1924.

Virginia Stowe Austin
Los Angeles

Registered this trademark, **Clippo,** for dolls in 1937.

Aux Rêves de l'Enfance
Paris

Established c. 1870, Aux Rêves de l'Enfance was a distributor of bisque-headed, kid-bodied dolls. Marks such as those illustrated here generally appeared on the dolls' chests or stomachs.

Averill Manufacturing Co.
New York City

The first company known to have manufactured and distributed the popular designs of Madame Georgene Averill, Averill Manufacturing was, at first (c. 1915), a family-run business, with the designer's husband and brother serving as its principals. While the firm was known to use other designers (including Grace Drayton), its most popular lines—**Madame Hendren** and **Life-Like**, later registered as **Lyf-Lyk**—were the creations of Mrs. Averill herself. Among the trade names attributed to Averill Manufacturing are the following (Madame Hendren appears most often in the firm's marks):

Baby Booful (1920)
Baby Brite (1924)
Baby Darling (1918)
Baby Dingle (1924)
Baby Virginia (1917)

Buddy Boy (1920)
Chocolate Drop (1923)
Cowboy (1916)
David (1918)
Dolly Dingle (1923)
Dolly Reckord (1922)
Gold Medal Baby (1924)
Gretchen (1916)
Halloween Dolls (1916)
Happy Cry (1924)
Indian Maid (1916)
Janie (1920)
Life-Like (1917)
Lullaby Baby (1924)
Lyf-Lyk (1917)
Madam(e) Hendren (1915—see marks; circular one registered 1922)
Madame Hendren's Life-Like Mama Dolls (1918)
Mama Doll (1918)
Mi-Baby (1924)
Miss U.S.A. (1917)
Neutrality Jim (1916)
Peggy (1920)
Pharaoh (1923)
Polly (1920)
Preparedness Kids (1916)
Princess Angeline (1917)
Rock-a-Bye Baby (1920)
St. Patrick (1922)
Sis (1924)
Softanlite (1921)
Soldier Boys (1916)
Sonny (1920)
Turtle Brand (1916)
U-Shab-Ti (1923)
Uncle Sam Jr. (1917)
Virginia Dare (1917)

According to Dorothy Coleman, the Averills left Averill Manufacturing by the early 1920s to found a new company called Madame Georgene Inc., which acted as both a wholesaler and a retailer. Georgene Averill's most popular dolls remained with Averill Manufacturing; new lines, including **Wonder Mama Dolls** (1922), were introduced by Madame Georgene. The Averill situation is complicated further by Coleman's documentation of a third firm, Paul Averill Inc. (1920-1924), which was thought to have made and sold Georgene Averill's designs. Perhaps Paul Averill Inc. became the manufacturing arm for the talented family after 1920, while Madame Georgene Inc. handled distribution. Georgene Averill herself registered several trade names after 1920, including Mak-a-Doll (1922). In any event, Madame Georgene Inc. advertised a number of dolls in the early 1920s, including Betty (1920), Billy (or Billie) Boy (1920), Master Bubbles (1922), Mistress Bubbles (1922), Wonder (reg. 1923, used since 1920), and Wonder Mama Dolls (1922).

Copr. by Georgene Averill 1005/3652 Germany

B

Babs Mfg. Corp.
Philadelphia

Patented a non-mechanical walking doll in 1919.

Baby Phyllis Doll Co.
Brooklyn, New York

The German porcelain factory of Armand Marseille supplied bisque heads for this firm's Baby Phyllis line of dolls beginning in about 1925; thus the allusion to Germany on the mark. In addition, however, the Brooklyn company's Baby Phyllis Mama Doll line included infants and adult dolls from its inception in 1919; J. Bouton & Co. was one of its distributors.

BABY PHYLLIS
Made in Germany

Bähr & Pröschild
Ohrdruf, Germany

Founded in 1871, the Bähr & Pröschild porcelain factory made both bisque and celluloid dolls, including the all-bisque "bathing dolls" or Frozen Charlottes popular in the latter years of the 19th century. In addition to the company's distinctive marks, shown here, its dolls can sometimes be recognized by their sharply slanted eyebrows, more typical of Oriental than of Anglo-Saxon features.

Bähr & Pröschild mold numbers include: 201, 204, 207, 209, 212, 213, 217, 219, 220, 224, 225, 226, 227, 230, 239, 244, 245, 247, 248, 251, 252, 253, 259, 260, 261, 263, 264, 265, 269, 270, 273, 275, 277, 278, 281, 283, 285, 287, 289, 292, 297, 300, 302, 305, 306, 309, 313, 320, 321, 322, 323, 324, 325, 330, 340, 342, 343, 348, 350, 374, 375, 376, 378, 379, 380, 381, 389, 390, 393, 394, 424, 425, 441, 482, 499, 500, 520, 525, 526, 529, 531, 535, 536, 537/2 033, 539/2 023, 541, 546, 549, 554, 557, 568, 571, 581, 584, 585, 600, 604, 619, 624, 640, 641, 642, 643, 644, 645, 646, 678, 707, and 799.

Dating Bähr & Pröschild heads is relatively easy. The firm began to use its BP initials about 1895. At the turn of the century, the mark included crossed swords. About 1919 the heart was used (just after the factory's purchase by Bruno Schmidt, whose trademark it originally was). The trademark **Buporit**, for celluloid dolls, was registered in 1909.

Baker & Bennett Company
New York City

A distributor and later a manufacturer as well, Baker & Bennett was established in 1902. Among the dolls it advertised were **The Spearmint Kid** (1915), **Zaiden** dolls (1916), and **Killblues** (1910), a name which was also used as the firm's trademark, along with its **double B initials**.

Ernst Ballu
Paris

A distributor of dolls established in 1890, Ballu registered **Bébé Olga** as a trademark for a *bébé incassable.*

BÉBÉ OLGA

BÉBÉ-OLGA

Martha Battle
Chattanooga, Tennessee

Registered the trademark **Evangeline** for dolls in 1937.

Bauer & Richter, Inc.
Stadtroda, Germany

Established by 1921, Bauer & Richter used no recognizable mark on its porcelain and celluloid babies, children, and mama dolls. The firm did, however, register several trademarks in 1922, including, **Asador**, **Herzkäferchen** (heart beetle), and **Mein Kleiner Schlingel** (My Little Rascal).

Karl Baumann
Ueberlingen, Germany

Baumann's dolls have composition bodies, bisque heads, and sleeping eyes. Some made around 1922 are marked KB-7½.

Emil Bauersachs
Sonneberg, Germany

The elaborate mark of Emil Bauersachs appeared on bisque-headed character babies and dolls with ball-jointed bodies. The firm, established in 1882, registered the name **Caprice** as a trademark for its character dolls nearly three decades later.

Bawo & Dotter
Karlsbad, Bohemia

As was the case with many doll manufacturers, Bawo & Dotter was first established as a porcelain factory (1838) and is not thought to have begun production of dolls and doll parts until several decades later. The firm established an import branch in New York in the 1860s and a second factory in Limoges, France, in 1872. Bawo & Dotter's marks appeared on both china and bisque-headed dolls; among the trademarks registered were **Barclay Baby Belle** (1908) and **Baby Belle** (1906). According to Dorothy Coleman, the New York company advertised the **Baby Belle** line as having been made in Waltershausen, though it is unclear whether it maintained a factory there as well.

0
Pat. Dec. 7/80

B&D

B&D
Lt∂

Bayerische Celluloidwarenfabrik
Nuremberg, Germany

Founded in 1897, the firm manufactured celluloid dolls. It registered the trademarks **Kleiner Spatz** and **Cleo** for two character dolls in 1926.

Iris Beaumont
Berlin

Registered **I.B.** as a trademark in 1922 for her art dolls, tea-cosy dolls, character dolls, and play dolls.

The Beaver Co.
Beaver Falls and Buffalo, New York; Ottawa, Ontario; and London

Registered **Beaverbilt** and **Beaverbeast** as trademarks for wooden dolls, 1916.

Richard Beck & Co.
Waltershausen, Germany

In 1903, the company advertised leather dolls, ball-jointed dolls, dolls' heads of porcelain, wood and papier mâché; and various doll parts.

Henri Bellet
Paris

Registered **Poupard Art** as a trademark for art dolls in 1919.

" POUPARD " ART

Belleville & Cie.
Paris

Registered **Mystère** in 1920 as a trademark for dolls, dolls' heads, and mechanisms for moving eyes.

MYSTÈRE

Belton & Jumeau
(see Jumeau)

Erich von Berg
Steinbach, Germany

All that is known of Berg is his mark and the fact that he was working in Germany around 1930.

EvB
Germany
1

Hermann von Berg
Köppelsdorf, Germany

Berg founded the firm in 1904 as a factory for doll wigs and eyes. Eventually production was expanded to include celluloid dolls' heads and jointed dolls. By 1922, the

H.v.B
500/4

company was producing leather and porcelain doll bodies, and in 1931 it advertised a crawling, talking baby marked **Habeka.**

Sol Bergfeld & Son
New York City

Although Bergfeld is not known to have used any one mark or series of marks, the American manufacturer's output in the mid-1920s was impressive. Its dolls, distributed by Borgfeldt, were mostly part of a series called the **Storybook Line.** They included the following trade names, all introduced in 1925:

Babes in the Woods
Charlotte Doll (not part of the series)
Goldey Locks
Jack and Jill
Little Bo-Peep
Little Red Riding Hood
Mary and Her Garden
Mary and Her Little Lamb
Tom and the Pig

C. M. Bergmann
Waltershausen, Germany

Charles M. Bergmann spent twelve years learning the doll-making business under various manufacturers before launching his own company in 1889. The firm specialized in ball-jointed composition bodies, to which were added bisque heads from the

C.M.Bergmann
Waltershausen
Germany
1916
9

C.M.B.
SIMON & HALBIG
Eleonore

HALBIG

C.M.BERGMANN

S&H

S&H

C.M.B

factories of Simon & Halbig, Armand Marseille, and other German makers. Bergmann's dolls were distributed in the United States by Louis Wolf, who registered several Bergmann trademarks in America, among them **Cinderella Baby** (1892), **Baby Belle** (1913), and the best-known **Columbia**, a line of both kid-body and composition-body dolls introduced in 1904.

Simon & Halbig heads supplied to Bergman include those marked Eleanore and Columbia, as well as a head with mold number 615.

S. Bergmann Jr. & Co.

Neuhaus, Germany

Porcelain factory founded in 1920; produced dolls' heads.

P
20/0
Germany
N

Carl Bergner

Sonneberg, Germany

Established in 1890, this German manufacturer is thought to have specialized in multi-faced dolls. The simple mark illustrated here has been found on many two- and three-faced dolls manufactured in the early years of the 20th century; it is probable, though not certain, that the mark was

Bergner's. One of the talking dolls positively attributed to Bergner is marked **450 dep.** Simon & Halbig made some of Bergner's two-faced and multi-faced doll heads.

Rolf Berlich

Charlottenburg, Germany

Rolf Berlich's firm, in existence by 1920, made cloth dolls and stuffed toys. Its circular trademark, registered in 1923, was impressed on a lead seal attached to the doll's hand.

Jacques Berner

Paris

Manufactured **Bébé Moujik**, 1888. The mark shown was affixed to the boxes containing his dolls.

MARQUE DÉPOSÉE
J B

Bernheim & Kahn

Paris

The **Etoile Bébé** and **Bébé Mondain** marks illustrated here are variants used by Bernheim & Kahn for its line of Parisienne bébés c. 1904. The **Etoile Bébé** mark has also been found flanked by five-pointed stars.

ETOILE BÉBÉ

BéBé ꙨONDAIN

Julius Bernhold
Paris

Registered **Nini Kaspa** as a trademark for composition art dolls in 1912.

NINI KASPA

René Bertrand
Paris

Registered **Gaby** as a trademark for dolls in 1923.

GABY

Bertoli Frères
Marseilles

Idéal Bébé was registered by Bertoli Frères in 1895. Unfortunately, little is known about the doll or dolls it was used to identify.

IDÉAL BÉBÉ

Bester Doll Manufacturing Co.
Bloomfield (and Newark), New Jersey

While it is probable that Bester created a doll especially for distribution by

BESTER DOLL C?
BLOOMFIELD

Morimura Brothers, most of the firm's output was sold direct to the trade during its brief existence (1919-1921).

L. Bierer
Sonneberg and Fürth, Germany

Founded in 1845, the firm was still making dolls in the 1920s, though it is probable that its bisque heads were purchased from Theodor Recknagel.

Fritz Bierschenk
(see E. Escher, Jr.)

Binder & Cie.
(see Société Binder & Cie.)

Gebrüder Bing
Nuremberg, Germany

Later known as Bing Werke (which, starting in 1920, used its initials as its mark), Gebrüder Bing was founded in 1882 and became one of Germany's most successful toy manufacturers, with branch offices scattered across the face of the globe. In addition to the mark shown here, Bing also used the initials **G.B.N.** on its variety of babies, children, and lady dolls. Among the names it registered were **Sunshine Girl**, **Sunshine Kid**, and **Pitti-Bum**.

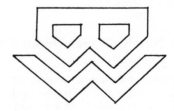

Bing Kunstlerpuppen- und Stoffspielwarengesellschaft

Nuremberg, Germany

The firm, made part of the Bing concern in 1921 when Gebrüder Bing absorbed the Albert Schlopsnies factory, produced art dolls, some with the trademark shown here (1925). The company went bankrupt in 1932.

John Bing Company

New York City

The exclusive American and Canadian representatives for Gebrüder Bing, John Bing also acted as agent for Kämmer & Reinhardt and Heinrich Handwerck, among other German firms. In addition, in the mid-1920s the firm advertised American dolls.

Bing Werke

(see Gebrüder Bing)

Bisc Novelty Manufacturing Co.

East Liverpool, Ohio

This midwestern firm was among the first to manufacture high-quality bisque dolls' heads entirely of American materials. The company's founder and designer, **Ernst Reinhardt,** was acknowledged in its mark.

$$H3$$
Reinhardt
East Liverpool
Ohio

Made in USA
Reinhardt
Pat.✦.Sep
Sh.18
Bisc Novelty Mfg. Co
East Liverpool Ohio

Blossom Products Corp.

Allentown, Pennsylvania

Registered **Quints** as a trademark for dolls in 1936.

Ernst Bohne

Rudolstadt, Germany

While the bisque dolls' heads from the Ernst Bohne factory can be identified by the anchor mark shown here, it is possible that the initials **E.B.**, also attributed to the French firms E. Balland Fils and Barrois, could have been used by the German maker as well.

Bonin & Lefort Cie.
Paris

Registered the trademark **Gaby, Ninon, Select,** and the circular mark shown in 1923; registered **Joli Bébé** and **Mon Baby** in 1927.

NINON

SELECT

GABY

MØN BABY

JOLI BÉBÉ

Claude Valéry Bonnal
Vincennes, France

Entirely concerned with the manufacture of *bébés incassable* (literally, "indestructible babies"), Bonnal's factory was established in 1898. In addition to the marks shown, registered trademarks included **Le Spécial, L'Unique,** and **Le Radieux** (all dating from 1904).

BÉBÉ L'UNIQUE
BÉBÉ LE RADIEUX
BÉBÉ LE SPÉCIAL
BÉBÉ LE PETIT FRANÇAIS
BÉBÉ LE GLORIEUX

George Borgfeldt & Company
New York City

George Borgfeldt was a talented businessman and entrepreneur whose company was responsible for commissioning two of the most successful dolls ever made: Rose O'Neill's **Kewpie** and Grace Storey Putnam's **Bye-Lo.** His early genius (in the 1880s) was in recognizing that there could be a sizeable American market for German and French dolls and in setting up salesrooms to display samples of particularly fine ones so that orders could be taken on the spot. Between 1881 (when Borgfeldt established his distribution company in New York) and 1887, he succeeded to the extent that he was able to open no fewer than eight branch offices in other countries—three of them in Germany. Borgfeldt worked with Simon & Halbig, Armand Marseille, and other large German firms, whom he commissioned to manufacture bisque heads to his specifications. It is generally agreed that the initials **G.B.** incised on dolls' heads in addition to the mark of the maker indicate the relationship. In addition, Borgfeldt acted as distributor for many American and Japanese manufacturers, as well as for Jeanne Orsini, an American designer whose character dolls were quite popular during the 1920s (see separate listing). Among the trade names registered by Borgfeldt for the dolls it represented were:

Alma (1900—see mark)
Tommy Atkins (1914)
Baby Belle (1907—see mark)
Baby Bo-Kaye (1926)
Baby Smiles (1926)
Bedtime (1923—see mark)
Betsy (1923)
Bettijak (1914)
Big Value/Knock About (1915—see mark)
Bonnie Babe (1926)
Bringing Up Father (1924)
Butterfly (1913)
Bye-Lo-Baby (1923—see mark)
Carrie (1913)
Celebrate (1895)
Charlie Carrot (1928)

Com-A-Long (1920)
Jackie Coogan (1925)
Cubist (1913)
Daisy (1923—see mark)
Dancing Kewpie Sailor (1922—see marks)
Defense (1916—see mark)
Didi (1922)
Dotty (1913)
Dotty Darling (1914)
Elsi (1898)
Em-Boss-O (1917)
Felix (1924—see mark)
Fingy-Legs the Tiny Tot (1912)
Florodora (1905—see mark)
Gladdie (1929)
Happifat (1913)
Happy Hooligan (1923—see mark)
Hi-Way Henry (1926)
Hollikid (1917—see mark)
The International Doll (1898—see mark)
Irvington (1910)
The Jolly Jester (1927)
Jolly Kids (1913)
Juno (1904)
Just Me (1929)
Kewpie (1913—see marks)
Kidlyne (1906)
Ko-ko (1925)
Lilly (1913)
Little Annie Rooney (1925)
Little Bright Eyes (1912)
Little Miss Sunshine (1913)
Little Sister (1914)
Lotta Sun (1920—see mark)
Mama's Angel Child (1914)
Mimi (1922)
Minnie Spinach (1928)
Miss Yankee (1919—see mark)
My Dearie (1908)
My Girlie (1913—see mark)
My Playmate (1907)
Nifty (1923—see mark)
Nobbikid (1915—see mark)
Paddy Potato (1926)
Pansy Doll (1910—see mark)
Peakies (1915—see mark)
Peero (1913)
Peter Rabbit Acrobat (1923—see mark)
Playmate (1918)
Powerful Katrinka (1923)
Preshus (1917)

Pretty Peggy (1908)
Princess (1898—see marks)
Prize Baby (1914)
Puddin Head (1923)
Reg'lar Fellers (1922)
Rosemarie (1923)
Betsy Ross (1924)
September Morn (1914)
Skating Charlotte (1915)
The Skipper (1923)
Skookum (1915—see mark)
Splashme (1919—see mark)
Story Book Dolls (1925)
Sugar Plum (1922)
Teenie Weenie (1922)
Tiny Tots (1912)
Tiss Me (1919—see mark)
Tommy Turnip (1928)
Tootsie (1906)
Tumble-Bo (1920—see mark)
UWanta (1899)
Virginia Ginny for Short (1927)
Vivi (1922)
Whatsamatter (1924)
Willy (1913)
Winkie (1919—see mark)
Xtra (1902)

BEDTIME

DANCING KEWPIE SAILOR

DEFENSE

HÓLLIKID

HAPPY HOOLIGAN

KEWPIE

LOTTA-SUN

MISS YANKEE

My Girlie
III.
Germany

NIFTY

Pansy.
IV.

Peakies

Peter Rabbit Acrobat

Princess
1
Germany

ARTISTE

SPLASHME

TUMBLE-BO

WINKIE

Jean Born & Cie.
(see Francis Thieck and Jean Born & Cie.)

Boston Pottery Company
Boston

Bisque-headed dolls incised **B.P.D.Co.**, along with **Made in Boston, Mass.//U.S.A.** are thought to have been made by this firm during the early 1920s.

A. Bouchet
London

The entwined initials illustrated have been attributed to this mid-19th century manufacturer, but there are other firms that used similar marks.

Ad. Bouchet
Paris

Ad. Bouchet's success as a manufacturer is corroborated by the records of the 1889 and '95 Paris Expositions and those at Rouen and Brussels in the next two successive years, all of which cite the firm as a silver- or gold-medal winner. Among the trade names registered were **Bébé Dormeur** (1898), **Bébé Géant** (1889), **Bébé Hamac** (1898), **Bébé Parlant** (1898), **Bébé Tête Mobile** (1895), **Gentil Bébé** (1895), **Le Séduisant** (1898), and **L'Indestructible** (1895).

A·D
BOUCHET
O

J. Bouton & Co.
New York City

Established in 1919, this American distributor advertised its **Jay-Bee** line of dolls, which included **Baby Bunting** (1925), **Baby Phyllis** (1925), **Bouton's Dancing Girls** (1923), **Miss Josephine** (1919), and **Peter Pan Doll** (1924).

Resi Brandl
Berlin

Registered **Bufli** as a trademark for its cloth dolls and animals in 1924.

BUFLI

Emma L. Bristol
Providence, Rhode Island

The firm, which is known to have made composition dolls, was extant during the final two decades of the 19th century, and perhaps longer.

BRISTOL'S UNBREAKABLE DOLL
273 HIGH St. PROVIDENCE, R.I.

Amilcare Brogi
Coeuilly-Champigny, France

Registered **Clelia** as a trademark for dolls in 1928.

Mayotta Browne
San Francisco

Browne registered **Otsy-Totsy Dolls** as a trademark for her rag dolls in 1922.

Bru Jne. & Cie.
Paris

There can be no doubt that the delicately modeled, limpid-eyed bébés produced by Bru during the last quarter of the 19th century are among the most treasured assets of collectors today. In addition to its fame as one of the finest manufacturers of porcelain dolls' heads, however, Bru was a pioneer in mechanical dolls; among the other materials used in the creation of its dolls were wood, rubber, and papier mâché. Bru used a variety of marks on its dolls, some as simple as the semicircle and dot shown here; others, more elaborate.

Any doll found with these marks can be dated prior to 1899, the year in which S.F.B.J. was formed (Bru was a charter member of the new firm). The trademark **Bébé Bru** (1866) was used both for stationary dolls and for mechanical ones. Among the names also registered for dolls which walked, talked, ate, and simulated other lifelike activities were **Bébé Gourmand** (1881), **Bébé Petit Pas** (Baby Small Step—1891), **Bébé Teteur** (1878), **Le Dormeur** (1885), and **Surprise Doll** (1867).

V. M. Bruchlos
Eisfeld, Germany

Valentin Moritz founded the firm in 1902 and made dressed mechanical dolls.

Albert Brückner
Jersey City, New Jersey

Brückner patented a rag doll in 1901, as his mark suggests. More than two decades later (1925), his sons had taken over the business and registered a new line of rag dolls which they called **Dollypop Dolls.**

PAT'D. JULY 8ᵀᴴ 1901

Marguerite Brunot
Algiers

Registered her trademark for dolls in 1918.

A. Bucherer
Amriswil, Switzerland

Bucherer's mark appears on a variety of metal-bodied dolls with composition heads modeled to represent amusing characters of the 1920s, including policemen, firemen, clowns, and comic-strip characters.

MADE IN
SWITZERLAND
PATENTS
APPLIED FOR

Oskar Büchner
Ebersdorf, Germany

This German doll manufacturer flourished in the mid-1920s.

H. Bühl & Söhne
Grossbreitenbach, Germany

This porcelain factory is known to have manufactured dolls' heads during the last three decades of the 19th century but was primarily a producer of bathing dolls in the 20th.

Theodor Buschbaum
Wallendorf, Germany

Founded in 1859, this doll firm made porcelain dolls, nanking dolls, bathing dolls, and dressed dolls through the first three decades of the 20th century.

Wilhelm Buschow
Dresden, Germany

A celluloid and rubber factory established in 1896, Buschow manufactured celluloid jointed dolls, character babies, dolls'-house dolls, and various doll parts. The 1929 trademark shown incorporates the words **Mein Herzenskind** (My Sweetheart).

Buschow & Beck
Reichenbach, Germany

Known primarily for its metal dolls' heads, Buschow & Beck also produced heads of celluloid, though the most collectible of its dolls remain the brass Minervas which were registered in 1900 (and also made by A. Vischer & Co.). After 1907, the brass was replaced by a combination of celluloid and washable enamel designed to overcome the chief drawback of metal heads: chipping and flaking. The name **Minerva** was generally embossed on the front of the breast plate as shown here, making identification a fairly simple matter. **Germany** sometimes appeared on the back of the metal-head shoulder plate.

GERMANY
3

Butler Brothers
Sonneberg, Germany

Butler Brothers was founded in 1877 as both a doll manufacturer and distributor; by 1886, its catalogue listed a wide variety of wax, china, "French bisque," and kid-body dolls. Throughout the latter part of

the 19th century, Butler Brothers was known as one of the largest distributors in America, with main offices in New York City. Among the trade names Butler used in the early 1900s were **Marvel**, which identified the firm's line of kid-body dolls, and **Pet Name**, china heads with the individual doll's names—**Agnes, Bertha, Dorothy, Ethel, Helen,** and **Marion** among them—molded on the breast plate. Other dolls distributed by Butler Brothers included:

Baby Betty (1912)
Baby Bud (1915)
Baby Catherine (1918)
Banker's Daughter (1893)
Banner Kid Dolls (1893)
Crying Babies (1907)
Dolly Dainty (1910)
Dolly Varden (1906)
Favorite (1910)
Harlequin (1916)
Jeweled (1905)
Little Aristocrat (1893)
Little Beauty (1910)
May Queen (1910)
Miss Millionaire (1910)
Model (1900)
Nansen (1912)
Nemo (1910)
North Pole (1910)
Papa and **Mamma Talking Dolls** (1906)
Princess Eulalia (1893)
Rattle Head (1905)
Red Riding Hood (1907)
Russian Princess (1893)
Special (1893)
Sultana (1893)
Sunny Jim (1910)
Tam O'Shanter (1893)
Terror (1905)
Uncle Sam (1905)
Vassar (1912)
The Wide-Awake Doll (1913—see mark)

THE
"WIDE-AWAKE"
DOLL
REGISTERED
GERMANY

C

Cameo Doll Co.
New York City and Port Allegany, Pennsylvania

Founded by successful designer Joseph Kallus in 1922, the Cameo Doll Company manufactured composition and wooden dolls, including versions of Rose O'Neill's **Kewpie** (1922), Grace Storey Putnam's **Bye-Lo** (1924), and **Little Annie Roonie** (1925), which Kallus designed in conjunction with Jack Collins, the character's creator. While Kallus had a knack for working with other designers to create better and better versions of their ideas (his 1932 rendition of cartoonist Max Fleischer's **Betty Boop** was one of his best-selling creations), he created many popular designs of his own, many of

Germany.
LITTLE ANNIE ROONEY
REG. U.S. PAT. OFF
COPR. BY JACK COLLINS

Copr. by
J.L. Kallus
Germany
1394/30

which were distributed by Borgfeldt. (The mark shown often appeared on dolls he created.) Among the trade names he registered were:

Baby Adele (1930)
Baby Blossom (1927)
Baby Bo-Kaye (1926)
Bandmaster (Bandy—1935)
Betty Boop (1932)
Bozo (1928)
Canyon Kiddies (1927—designed by James Swinnerton)
Cookie (1941)
Crownie (1940)
Joy (1932)
Little Annie Rooney (1925)
Marcia (1933)
Margie (1929)
Pete the Pup (c. 1932)
Pinkie (1930)
Popeye (1932—licensed by King Features Syndicate)
Scootles (1930s)
Sissie (1928)

Canzler & Hoffmann
Berlin and Sonneberg, Germany

Begun as a distributor and exporter in 1906, Canzler & Hoffmann was making dolls by 1910. Its **Caho** trademark, taken from the first letters of the principals' names, was not registered until 1925. By 1930 the firm was advertising dolls of leather, celluloid, and a combination of the two materials.

Capo Di Monte
Naples, Italy

Noted for its exquisite porcelain for more than two centuries, Capo Di Monte almost assuredly made dolls' heads as well. The company's mark was often forged, however, and care should be taken to verify that dolls bearing the **crown and N** symbol are authentic.

Max Carl & Co.
Neustadt, Germany

In the 1890s, this German manufacturer produced jointed dolls bearing the mark shown here. The company is known to have made dolls' heads shortly after the turn of the century.

Robert Carl
Köppelsdorf, Germany

A producer of porcelain-headed dolls beginning in 1895, Robert Carl also used heads made by Armand Marseille for his specialty, mechanical dolls. Carl advertised features such as eyes that opened and shut, as well as talking dolls. He registered one trademark, **Mausi** (Mousie), in 1908. Frickmann & Lindner of Köppelsdorf bought the Carl factory in 1911, though the Carl name was used for more than a decade after the sale. The **RC** within the circle was Carl's own mark; the second mark shown was used by his successors after 1926. In 1913, Carl became co-owner of Porzellanfabrik Mengersgereuth, which see.

Germany·
1400/4

Jean Carles
Nice, France

Registered his trademark for dolls in 1926.

Adrien Carvaillo
Paris

Registered **La Vénus** as a trademark for rag dolls, 1923.

LA VÉNUS

Catterfelder Puppenfabrik
Catterfeld, Germany

Established in 1906, Catterfelder Puppenfabrik made bisque-headed composition dolls, specializing in baby dolls (and later character babies) and jointed dolls. It was known to have used the two marks pictured here. In addition, Catterfelder Puppenfabrik registered several trademarks for its dolls: **My Sunshine** (Mein Sonnenschein) and **Little Sunshine** (Kleiner Sonnenschein). Since bisque heads have been found with the Kestner mark **K & Co.**, in addition to the Catterfelder mark, it is sur-

C.P.
208/34 S
Deponiert

mised that Kestner made some of the heads used on the Catterfelder dolls.

Among the mold numbers thought to have been used on Catterfelder dolls are: 200, 205, 206, 207, 208, 209, 218, 219, 220, 262, 263, 264, 270, 1100, 1200, and 1357.

Madame E. Cayette
Paris

The five-pointed star and four-leaf clover shown were registered by Madame Cayette (née Marie Mommessin) in 1909. Among her trademarks, registered in the same year, were **Bébé Prophète**, **Bébé Oracle**, **La Fée au Gui**, **La Fée au Trèfle**, **La Fée aux Trèfles**, and **La Fée Bonheur**.

Cellba Celluloidwarenfabrik
Babenhausen, Germany

The firm produced celluloid dolls and doll parts during the mid-1920s.

Century Doll Co.
New York City

Century Doll Company, founded in 1909, was both a manufacturer and a distributor. Most of its marks, as indicated here, included the name **Century** or at least the initials **CDCO**, making identification a fairly simple matter. Century imported many of its heads from Kestner, as the **K** within

the diamond indicates. As distributors, the company arranged for exclusive American use of Kestner's crown trademark in 1925. Among the trade names of Century's dolls were the following:

Babette (1924)
Baby Shirley (1918)
Barbara (1924)
Blue Eyes (1921)
Brown Skin Dolls (1922)
The Century Doll (1909)
Clap Hands (1925)
Darky Dolls (1922)
Kuddle Kiddies (1922)
Marvel Mama Dolls (1923)
Mastercraft Babies (1918)
Quality Bilt (1918)
Sweetums (1925)
Wood-Bisk (1921)

Germany
CENTURY DOLL &.C⁰·

CENTURY DOLL C°
Kestner Germany

Chambon et Baye
France

In 1889, this firm made a three-faced

stuffed doll, the various faces manipulated by a handle under the doll's bonnet.

Chambre Syndicale des Fabricants de Jouets Français
Paris

A group of French toy manufacturers founded this syndicate in 1886; among its members were Pean (Frères), Henri Alexandre, Dehais, and Falck & Roussel.

Martha J. Chase
Pawtucket, Rhode Island

Inspired by an Izannah Walker rag doll that she had owned as a child, Mrs. Martha Jenks Chase made a soft, unbreakable, washable doll for her own children in the closing years of the 19th century. The result, the **Chase Stockinet Doll**, became an unexpected commercial success. Mrs. Chase, the wife of a physician, went on to make a wide variety of cloth dolls, including both adult and child-size "hospital dolls" used for training nurses. (The nurse caricature shown became her trademark). Among the most famous dolls Mrs. Chase created, inspired by Tenniel's illustrations, was her series of *Alice in Wonderland* characters. Sometimes the names were stitched on the dolls' collars; sometimes the Chase nurse trademark was stamped on the body; occasionally the dolls were un-

marked. The names of some of the Chase dolls were:

Alice-in-Wonderland (1905)
Bessy Brooks (1921)
Duchess (1921)
Frog Footman (1921)
Mammy Nurse (1905)
Pickaninnies (1921)
Silly Sally (1921)
Tommy Snooks (1921)
Tweedledum and Tweedledee (1921)
George Washington (1905)

M.J.C.
Stockinet Doll
Patent Applied For

PAWTUCKET, R.I.
MADE IN U.S.A.

Chauvière
(see Au Nain Bleu)

Veuve Clément
Paris

The Widow (fr. *Veuve*) Clément sold dolls in Paris in the 1870s; it is probable that she was a relative of Pierre Victor Clément, who made dolls of pressed leather, as her mark has been found stamped on leather-bodied dolls produced during the period when he worked.

Cocheco Manufacturing Co.
United States

During the early 1890s, designers Celia and Charity Smith and Ida Gutsell contributed their talents to this textile manufacturer, which printed their colorful patterns on yard goods distributed by Lawrence & Company of Boston, Philadelphia, and New York. Thus both firms appear on the Cocheco mark, printed next to the two-piece patterns which were designed to be cut out, stuffed, and sewn.

Coiffe
Limoges, France

Established in 1873, Coiffe was a porcelain manufacturer whose seven-pointed star appeared on the dolls' heads it produced. The firm underwent several changes of name: Coiffe, Inc. (1898); Coiffe, Couty & Cie. (1915); and Couty, Magne & Cie. (1920).

Colonial Toy Manufacturing Co.
New York City

All-composition dolls were the staple of this American manufacturer, which was established in 1915. For the first three years

of its existence, David Zaiden was its president, and Zaiden was often incised on dolls during that period. Among the dolls Colonial advertised were **Baby Cuddles** (1920), **Miss Colonial** (1918), **Mother Goose Hug-Me-Tight** (1916—designed by Grace Drayton), **Next-to-Nature** (1918), **Peachy Pets** (1919), and **Snowbird** (1917).

COLONIAL
DOLL
MADE IN
U.S.A.

Charles Colombo
New York City

Patented **Chubby** and **Ritzie** dolls in 1936.

Concentra
(see Gebrüder Bing, Kämmer & Reinhardt, Schutzmeister & Quendt, and Welsch & Co.)

Conta & Böhme
Pössneck, Germany

The porcelain factory was founded in 1790 and purchased by Ernst Conta and Christian Gotthelf Böhme in 1804. The firm specialized in bathing dolls and nanking dolls; according to Jürgen and Marianne Cieslik, its trademark, a shield with a knight's arm holding a sword, is found on the sole of the bathing doll's foot. The Ciesliks, with the assistance of Dorothy Coleman, surmise that a **V37** mark was used on dolls' heads about 1878; a third mark, **IX 36,** has also been found on Conta & Böhme heads.

Madame Coquillet
Paris

Registered the trademark **La Parisette** in 1918.

LA PARISETTE

Marius Cornet
Lyons, France

Registered the trademark **La Poupée Française** in 1914 for various sorts of dolls.

LA POUPÉE FRANÇAISE

Corona Pottery
(see S. Hancock & Sons)

Jeanne Cortot
Liège, Belgium

Cortot, maker of **Bébé Jeannette** dolls, registered a trademark for his product in 1915 and then again in 1922.

Cosman Frères
Paris

Cosman Frères was established in 1892 as a doll manufacturer specializing in bébés and dressed dolls. Among the firm's trademarks were **Bébé le Favori** and **Bébé Favori** (1892) and **Splendide Bébé** (1893), the last registered for a line of bisque-headed, jointed bébés and dolls. It also was known to have sold dolls under the trade names of **Bébé le Splendide** and **Bébé Prime** (both in 1892).

Bébé Favori

Bébé le Favori

Splendide Bébé

Madame Raymonde Couin
Paris

Registered **Kipmi** as a trademark for dolls in 1924.

KiPMi

Couty, Magne & Cie.
(see Coiffe)

Henry Cremer
London

From the early 19th century until the beginning of the 20th, Henry Cremer and, later, his son, were among London's most respected and successful doll merchants. They were known to have imported dolls from France (a Jules Steiner doll with the Cremer rectangular sticker has been identified). The oval mark shown here was used after about 1862.

Joseph Cronan
Portland, Oregon

Registered **Mazel Tov** as a trademark for dolls, 1916.

Madame Aline Crosier
Paris

Registered her trademark for dolls in 1917.

PARFAIT - BÉBÉ
PARIS
MANUFACTURE FRANÇAISE
DE POUPEES ET JOUETS

Cunique des Poupées
Lausanne, Switzerland

Little is known about this Swiss distributor, founded about 1910. The firm used a

sticker, illustrated here, which has been found on a Kämmer & Reinhardt doll.

Curnen & Steiner
New York City and Sonneberg, Germany

The company registered the trademark C.&S. for its dolls in 1898.

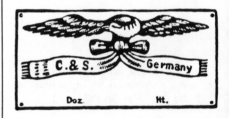

D

Dallwig Distributing Co.
Chicago

The firm manufactured dolls and special wigs for them which could be interchanged. Its trademark was registered in 1919.

.DALL WIG DOLL

Jules and Charles Damerval
Paris

Registered the trademark **Joli Bébé** in 1910

for dolls; are also thought to have used the name **Bébé Mignon**.

JOLI BÉBÉ

Danel & Cie.
Paris

The firm's main product was the **Paris Bébé**, a bisque-head doll introduced in 1889; it also registered **Bébé Français** as a trademark (1891) and made some of the earliest French black and mulatto dolls. It was taken over by Jumeau by 1896 but continued to manufacture dolls for some years thereafter.

**TETE DÉPOSÉE
PARIS-BÉBÉ**

**PARIS-BÉBÉ
Bréveté**

BÉBÉ FRANÇAIS

Robert Darcy
Paris

Registered his trademark in 1928; trademark used to designate dolls of "turtle leather."

Darrow Manufacturing Co.
Bristol, Connecticut

"Darrow dolls," as they were known, had cloth bodies and heads made of hand-painted, pressed rawhide. The firm made these distinctly American dolls for about a decade, beginning in 1866.

D'Autremont
Paris

This firm, founded in 1858, patented a rubber doll; its name was also stamped on the stomachs of some china-headed dolls with kid bodies. [The name of the company is sometimes spelled "D'Autrement".]

Davis & Voetsch
New York City

Sometimes known as the Dee Vee Doll Company, the firm registered **Dee Vee** as a trademark in 1923. Davis & Voetsch also distributed Heinrich Handwerck character dolls and stuffed dressed dolls made by Acme Toy Manufacturing Company.

Aline de Brzeska
Foutenay-sous-Bois, France

Registered **Lutetia** as a trademark for dolls, 1924.

Jeanne de Kasparek
Paris

Made art dolls and registered her trademark for them in 1922.

Max H. M. de la Ramée
Suresnes, France

Made unbreakable dolls and dolls' heads, 1917.

MA JOLIE

Marguerite de Raphelis-Soissan
Paris

Registered her trademark, Jeanne D'Arc, in 1920.

JEANNE D'ARC

Georges de Roussy de Sales
Belleville and Paris

Registered the trademarks **Liberty** (for dolls, 1918), **Expression** (for dolls' heads, 1918), **Modestes** and **Espiègles** (both for movable dolls' eyes, 1919).

LIBERTY

EXPRESSION

ESPIÈGLES

E. de Stoecklin and Gaston Manuel
Paris

Registered these three trademarks in 1920 for dolls.

POUPÉES DE PARIS

Les Poupées Parisiennes

LES POUPETTES

Renée de Wouilt
Paris

Registered her trademark for dolls in 1916.

Dean's Rag Book Co.
London

In 1903, Samuel Dean began to make rag cut-out dolls to be packaged in books. That method quickly gave way to selling the doll patterns on linen sheets, and eventually he offered pressed and stuffed dolls as well. The company expanded steadily, making more sophisticated dolls (jointed dolls, dolls with glass eyes, free-standing dolls) and a continually wider range of brands. In addition, it made costumes for its dolls. Its trademark, according to Constance King, consisted of "two dogs fighting over a rag book." King also notes that Dean's introduced an A1 label in 1923. Among the trade names the firm used were:

Betty Blue (c. 1910)
Big Baby (1910)
Bo-Peep (1913)
Buster Brown (c. 1922)
Captivating Cora (c. 1922)
Charlie Chaplin (c. 1922)
Cheeky Imp (1913)
Cinderella (1913)
Coogan Kid (c. 1922)
Cosy Kids (c. 1922)
Curly Locks (c. 1910)
Dinah Doll (1913)
George Robey (1923)
Life Size Baby Doll (c. 1903)
Little Sambo (1913)
Lucky Lockett (c. 1903)
Lucky Puck (c. 1910)
Lupino Lane (1937)
Mary Mary (c. 1922)
Master Sprite (1913)
Mickey Mouse (1937)
Miss Betty Oxo (1937)
Natty Nora (c. 1922)

Old King Cole (c. 1903)
Popeye (1937)
Red Riding-hood (1913)
Ta-Ta (c. 1922)
Tru-to-Life (c. 1917)

Yves de Villers & Co., Ltd.
New York City

Registered its trademark for dolls in 1926; indicated that it was to be used on labels.

Louis Dedieu
Paris

Registered **De Liauty** as a trademark for dolls in 1927.

DE LIAUTY

Dee Vee Doll Co.
(see Davis & Voetsch)

Dehais
(see Chambre Syndicale des Fabricants de Jouets Français)

E. Dehler
Coburg, Germany

This manufacturing and export firm was founded in 1866. In the first two decades of the 20th century it produced various types of dolls, including character babies,

dressed and undressed wooden dolls, and jointed dolls.

Louis Delachal
Paris

Starting in 1890, Delachal manufactured **Bébé Caoutchouc**, a line of rubber babies and dolls.

B. Delacoste & Cie.
(see B. Derolland)

Henri Delcroix
Montreuil, France

In 1887, Delcroix registered these four marks, which were intended to be stamped on dolls' heads.

.PARIS

PAN

PARIS

GD HD

PARIS

Sophia E. Delavan
Chicago

In 1916, Delavan began making dolls and doll wigs; among her first dolls were **War Nurse** and **War Orphan** (1917), named in acknowledgment of World War I. After the war (in 1921), she registered a line of **Buds** and **Buddies** rag dolls; their names included: **American Rose Bud, Buddie Clown, Greenwich Village Bud, Holland Bud, Rags Bud, Scotch Bud Golf Beauty,** and **Student.**

Delly-Puppenfabrik
Stuttgart, Germany

In the mid-1920s, this firm produced soft stuffed art dolls dressed in felt.

Madame Demarest
Clefs, France

Mme. Demarest affixed her trademark (registered in 1908) to boxes and other packing materials containing her dolls.

B. Derolland
Paris

One of the largest French producers of rubber dolls, Derolland founded his company in 1878 and produced a wide variety of dolls for a number of years thereafter. The second of the two marks shown was used

after 1921 by Derolland's successor, B. Delacoste & Cie.

Alexandrine D'Erophine
Paris

D'Erophine's trademark, registered in 1886, was to be affixed to her dolls; it was printed in a variety of sizes and colors.

Mademoiselle Desaubliaux
Boulogne-sur-Seine, France

Registered the trademark **Gallia** for dolls in 1915.

GALLIA

Hubert des Loges
Paris

Registered his trademark for dolls in 1916.

Josef Deurlein Nachf.
Nuremberg, Germany

In 1907, this firm registered a trademark for **Hercules** brand toys made of felt and leather; in 1913, it used the **Iden** trademark. The marks shown date from 1907.

Deutsche Kolonial-Kapok-Werke-AG
Berlin, Potsdam, and Württemberg

Advertised **Dekawe** — soft, stuffed animal toys that could be immersed in water—in 1925.

Diamond Pottery Co.
Hanley, England

Manufactured bisque dolls' heads for English dolls; used the mark **D.P. Co.** beginning in 1908.

The Doll Craft Co.
Brooklyn, New York

Registered **Cradoll** as a trademark for rag dolls in 1922.

Domec Toys Inc.
New York City

Domec Toys, established in 1924, began to manufacture an infant doll, **Kradle Babe,** in competition with Borgfeldt's best-selling Bye-Lo. Borgfeldt sued, claiming that the similarities between the two were an infringement of its copyright; Domec lost and ceased production of Kradle Babe, but continued with another line named **Dolls of Character.**

Dornheim, Koch, & Fischer
Gräfenroda, Germany

Founded in 1856 as a porcelain factory producing animal heads, the firm manufactured dolls' heads from c. 1880 until 1913.

Julius Dorst
Sonneberg, Germany

The very successful doll firm of Julius Dorst began as a children's drum factory, owned by Dorst's father-in-law. Dorst took over the firm in 1865 and expanded production to include various wooden toys and dolls. During its last decade, in the 1920s, it manufactured wooden toys exclusively. Among some of Dorst's innovations were a spring-loaded device to change doll heads and dolls that said "Mama" and "Papa" while swinging their heads.

Germaine Douche
Paris

Registered **Colette** and **Puppet's Mary** as trademarks in 1928.

Isidore Dreifuss
Strasbourg, France

Registered the trademark **La Poupée Idéale** for dolls in 1921.

Cuno & Otto Dressel
Sonneberg, Germany

This German firm, founded in the 1700s, is the oldest doll manufacturer for which reasonably accurate records exist. The Dressels of the 18th century dealt in small goods, including toys, and in 1789 were included in the group of companies granted exclusive trade rights in Sonneberg. The firm passed from one generation of Dressels to the next; in 1873 it became known as Cuno & Otto Dressel. The partnership was immensely successful; large quantities of its dolls were exported to America (many of them distributed by Butler Brothers). Cuno & Otto Dressel did not manufacture all of its dolls in its own factories, however. It ordered heads from Armand Marseille, Simon & Halbig, Gebrüder Heubach, and other German makers as well.

Mold numbers attributed to Dressel include 1348, 1349, 1468, 1469, 1776, 1848, 1849, 1893, 1896, 1898, 1912, 1914, 1920, 1922, and 2736.

Simon & Halbig heads made for Dressel include mold numbers 1348, 1349, 1468, 1469, 1848, 1849, 1912, and 1920.

Its most famous trademark, **Holzmasse**, was registered in 1875; among the other trade names used were:

Admiral Dewey (1898)
Admiral Sampson (1898)
Bambina (1909)
Die Puppe der Zukunft (Doll of the Future) (1899)

Fifth Ave Dolls (1903)
Jutta (1906)
Jutta-Baby (1922)

1469
C.&O. Dressel.
Germany.
2.

1349
Dressel
S&H
8

1348
Jutta
S&H
16

Heubach-Köppelsdorf
Jutta-Baby
Dressel
Germany
1922
10.

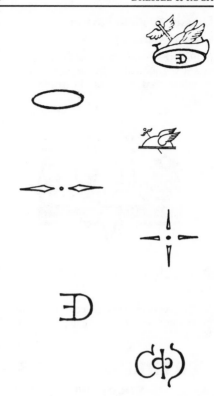

A.M.

C.O.D. 93·0·D.E.P.

Hugo Dressel
(see H. J. Leven)

Dressel & Koch
Köppelsdorf, Germany

Adolf Kratky founded the factory, and Hermann Dressel and Albing Koch became its owners in 1894. The company was dissolved in 1897, but during its brief tenure produced a variety of bisque dolls' heads.

C'Dep.　　　D&K N° ⅔

Dressel & Pietschmann
Coburg, Germany

In 1923, the firm of Dressel & Pietschmann advertised jointed dolls. Its factory also manufactured toys, as the trademark suggests.

Paul Dubois
Paris

In 1919, registered his trademark for dolls (a comment on the closing days of World War I).

ENTRÉE DES ALLIÉS
à STRASBOURG

Henriette Dunker
Hamburg, Germany

In 1923, Henriette Dunker registered the

trademark **Mein Stern** (my star) for dolls.

Madame Max Duran
Paris

Registered three trademarks for dolls in 1915.

DURAN MARX

Octave Durand
Colombes, France

Registered "**Tanagrette**" as a trademark in 1921.

" TANAGRETTE "

E

Berthold Eck
Unterneubronn, Germany

The Berthold Eck doll factory manufactured dolls, c. 1876-1882.

Gebrüder Eckardt
Oberlind, Germany

The brothers Ernst, Arthur, and Max Eckhardt founded the doll manufacturing and export firm c. 1920. Max Eckhardt became co-owner of the import house Strauss-Eckardt Co., Inc., of New York. The German firm exported exclusively, selling primarily to buyers in the United States and England. It produced various dolls with bisque heads, as well as doll accessories. One set of baby dolls with heads by Armand Marseille was named **Our Pet**, and the trademark GEO was registered in the 1930s for domestic trade.

Our Pet.
Germany.
3/0

540-4
GEO
5

Hermann Eckstein
Neustadt, Germany

In 1899, Hermann Eckstein began production of wax dolls for export to England. He expanded to papier-mâché babies, talking dolls, and jointed dolls. **Princess Sibylla**, modeled after the likeness of the German bride of Prince Gustov Adolf of Sweden, was introduced in 1932.

Edmund Edelmann
Sonneberg, Germany

Founded in 1903, this firm made a variety of celluloid and bisque dolls, including **Melitta** (whose bisque head was made by

Armand Marseille), **Mine**, and **Mona**, all introduced in 1922.

Melitta
A·Germany M.
12

Thomas Alva Edison
Orange, New Jersey

Edison, the inventor of the phonograph, had mixed success with his first talking doll (1879), a rather crude assembly of tin and wood. Ten years later, however, he introduced a more attractive version. It was composed of a metal torso which contained the phonograph and playing mechanism, wooden limbs, and a Simon & Halbig bisque head, marked with either mold number 719 or 917. Complete models are rare; they can be identified by the imprint on the mechanism, which reads "**Edison Phonograph Toy//Manufacturing Co.// New York**" and includes the patent dates.

R. Eekhoff
Groningen, Netherlands

The lady doll manufactured by Eekhoff c. 1894 depicted a married woman dressed in an old-fashioned country style; Eekhoff used a Simon & Halbig bisque head.

R.EEKHOFF
Groningen

Effanbee
New York City

Founded as Fleischaker & Baum in 1910 by partners Bernard E. Fleischaker and Hugo Baum, this extremely successful manufacturer registered its famous trademark, **Effanbee**, in 1913 and is more commonly known by that name. During the firm's first few years, it produced "unbreakable" composition dolls; by 1918 it had added stuffed-body dolls as well. One of Effanbee's often-used tag lines, **They Walk and They Talk**, was introduced in

1922; it was amended to **They Walk, They Talk, They Sleep** just a year later, even though, as Dorothy Coleman relates, many of the dolls on which the slogan is found did none of those things. Effanbee continues to make a wide variety of dolls to this day; among the most collectible of its dolls, however, were those manufactured prior to World War II. Some of their trade names follow:

Alice Lee (1924)
Baby Dainty (1912—see mark)
Baby Effanbee (1925)
Baby Grumpy (1914—see mark)
Barbara Lee (1924)
Beach Baby (1923)
Betty Bounce (1913)
Betty Lee (1924)
Billie (1924)
Bubbles (1925)
Christening Babies (1919)
Colleen Moore (c. 1930)
Columbia (1916)
The Doll with the Golden Heart (1923)
Dolly Dumpling (1918)
Dy-Dee Doll (1935)
The EFFanBEE Buttons Monk (1923—see mark)
French Baby (1918)
Gladys (1924)
Harmonica Joe (1924)
Honeybunch (1923)
I Say Papa (1921)
Joan (1924)
Johnny Tu-Face (1912)
Jumbo (1914)
Little Walter (1912)
Lovums (1918)
Mae Starr (1930)
Margie (1921)
Marilee (c. 1925)
Mary Ann (1923)
Mary Jane (1917)
Miss Coquette (Naughty Marietta) (1912)
Nancy Ann (1923)
New Born Baby (1925)
Pat-o-Pat (1925)
Patricia (1932)
Patsy (1927)
Patsy-Ann (c. 1930)
Patsy Tinyette (1933)
Peter (1924)
Popeye & Olyve Oyl (1935)

Reversible (1920)
Riding Hood Bud (1919)
Rose Marie (1925)
Rosemary (1925)
Salvation Army Lass (1921)
Anne Shirley (c. 1935)
Skippy (c. 1930)
Snow White (c. 1939)
Sugar Baby (1936)
They Walk and They Talk (1922)
They Walk, They Talk, They Sleep (1923)
Trottie Truelife (1921)
Uncle Sam (1916)
Valentine Bud (1919)
George and Martha Washington (c. 1940)

Christian Eichorn & Söhne
Steinach, Germany

Founded in 1860 by Max and Albert Eichorn, the firm became known as Christian Eichorn & Söhne in 1909. It produced porcelain dolls' heads, bathing dolls, and doll parts until c. 1930.

Eisenmann & Co.
Fürth, Germany and London

The firm was founded by Gabriel and Josef Eisenmann in 1881 as a housewares exporter; it did not begin to trade in dolls until 1895 nor to manufacture them until the early 20th century. Among the trademarks Eisenmann registered in London were **Beaky-Ba** (1913), **Bunny Hug** (1914), **Floatolly** (1914), **Hugmee** (1912), **Kiddieland** (1911), **Kwacky-Wack** (1912), **Little Pet** (1908), and **Toddles** (1912).

Germany
Einco

J. Eisenstaedt & Co.
(see Hermann Landshut & Co.)

Elektra Toy & Novelty Co.
New York City

The firm produced composition dolls beginning in 1912; many of its earliest dolls had flirting eyes. Among the trade names it advertised were:

Amy (1912)
Billy Boy (1912)
Chubby (1917)
The Favorite (1914)
Fritz, Mitzi (1913)
Goo Goo Eye Dolls (1912)
Jolly Jumps (1912)
Laurie (1912)
Margot, Frou Frou (1913)
Rosy-Posy (1917—see mark)
Suffragina (1914)
Tootsie Wootsie (1916)

ELEKTRA T.N.C. NY
COPYRIGHT

Elpikbien
Paris

Used a **wheel with spokes**, surrounded by C O, as a trademark, 1921.

Erste Nordhäuser Spielwarenfabrik
(see Hermann Wolf)

Erste Schleisische Puppenfabrik
(see Heinrich Schmuckler)

Erste Steinbacher Porzellanfabrik
Steinbach, Germany

Founded in 1900 as Max Kiesewetter & Co., the company manufactured bisque dolls' heads from 1902 until c. 1937, except for the years during and after World War I (1914-1922). Because ownership of the factory was transferred several times during its years of operation, the marks incised on the heads vary significantly. During the tenure of Hugo Wiefel (1912), the company was known as Wiefel & Co., and the **W & Co.** mark was used on socket

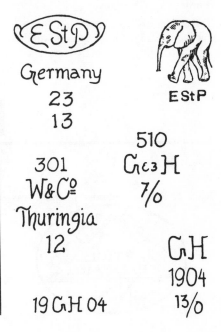

heads marked 121 and 131. The **elephant** trademark and initials **EStP** were used after 1923, when the firm was known as Erste Steinbacher Porzellanfabrik. The **GH** was introduced after 1930, when Gustav Heubach took over. Known numbers incised were 510, 1904, 1905, and 1906.

E. Escher, Jr.
Sonneberg, Germany

Founded in 1880 by E. Escher, Jr., the firm manufactured and exported papier-mâché doll heads, jointed dolls, doll bodies, and by 1903 was advertising dolls of leather, felt, and wood. Fritz Bierschenk became its new owner in 1905 and the firm was renamed for him, though it continued to use the Escher trademark (originally registered in 1880).

Trade Mark

J. G. Escher & Söhn
Sonneberg, Germany

This doll factory was founded in 1790; during the late 1890s it advertised wooden dolls and by 1914 was manufacturing celluloid dolls, babies, and doll parts. Its trademark was registered in 1914.

European Doll Manufacturing Co.
New York City

In the early 1920s this firm, which used **Eur** as a trade name, advertised unbreakable character dolls made in the United States.

Laura J. Eyles
Chicago

Registered **Tut Sye Amen** as a trademark for dolls in 1923.

F

Falck & Roussel
Paris

Falck & Roussel, founded in 1880, was

among the first French companies to make composition bébés. The firm registered its **F.R.** and **Bébé Mignon** trademarks in 1885; several million Bébé Mignons were manufactured between 1886 and 1902.

Famous Doll Studio
New York City

Founded in 1906, this doll manufacturer advertised its **Sani-Doll** in 1916.

M. Fauche
Paris

Registered **Manos.** as a trademark for dolls in 1916.

MANOS.
MARQUE DEPOSÉE

Faultless Rubber Co.
Ashland, Ohio

Between 1916 and 1922, the firm produced a variety of molded rubber dolls. The trade names included: **Billy Boy** (1918), **Boy Scout** (1918), **Fairy** (1918), **Miss Sunshine** (1918), **Nurse** (1918), **Pat-Biddy** (1920), **Sailor Boy** (1918), and **Sweetie** (1917).

Carl Feiler & Co.
Jena, Germany

Produced leather and jointed dolls, c. 1900-1903.

Fischer, Naumann & Co.
Ilmenau, Germany

This firm, which also manufactured terra cotta, began manufacturing dolls by 1852. Its output included doll parts, leather dolls, and porcelain dolls. The **FNI** trademark was registered in 1876; the elaborately entwined **FNC** has been found on leather dolls; and the last trademark shown was registered in 1927. Fischer, Naumann & Co. survived under various managements well into the 1930s.

Fleischaker & Baum
(see Effanbee)

Fleischmann & Bloedel
Fürth and Sonneberg, Germany; Paris; and London

Soon after its founding in 1873 by Saloman Fleischmann and Jean Bloedel, this German manufacturer became an important doll supplier to France, producing various walking, talking, nodding, and kissing dolls. In 1890, the trademark **Eden Doll** was registered to signify a wide range of dolls, followed by **Bébé Triomphe** in 1898. Simon & Halbig made bisque heads marked **DEP** for Fleischmann & Bloedel which were specifically intended for the French market. Because of its success in that market, Fleischmann & Bloedel became a founding member of S.F.B.J. in 1899.

Joseph Berlin, who took over the firm's German operations in 1905, expanded production to include felt and plush toys and character dolls; he registered the trademark **Michu** in 1914. The firm closed in 1926.

„*Michu*"

EDEN BEBE

Eden-Bébé

A. Fleischmann & Craemer
Sonneberg, Germany

Founded in 1844 as A. Fleischmann & Co. the firm manufactured 300,000 papier-mâché doll heads a year by 1851. In 1881 the original A. Fleischmann & Co. closed and was replaced by two new firms—the identically named A. Fleischmann & Co., owned by Adolf Fleischmann and Carl Craemer, and Augus Luge & Co. The new Fleischmann registered its square trademark (1881) for dolls, toys, and various glasswares. The firm gradually moved under the control of the Craemers, specializing in papier-mâché dolls and character dolls. (The rectangular **AF & C** mark is found on papier-mâché heads.) The circular **AF & C** mark was introduced in the 1920s, some years after Carl Craemer and his son-in-law had founded a new firm, Porzellanfabrik Mengersgereuth. The firm is still in operation in Nuremberg.

AF.&C.
Superior
2018

Florig & Otto
Dresden, Germany

Founded in 1920, Florig & Otto produced ball-jointed dolls in wood and cloth; registering the trademarks **Florigotto** (1920), **FO** (1921), and **Puck** (1923). The company was in operation until c. 1925.

Albert Förster
Neustadt, Germany

Produced dolls in the late 1920s.

Gustav Förster
Neustadt, Germany

August Förster founded the firm in 1905. His son, Gustav, took it over by 1925, when it was producing various types of dolls, including character dolls, toddlers, and bent-limb babies. (Gustav's trademark is shown.)

Blanche Fouillot

Paris

Made dolls under the trade name L'Idéal, beginning in 1906.

L'Idéal

Mme. Consuélo Fould

Paris

Registered **Les Victorieuses** as a trademark for dolls in 1919.

Johannes Franz

Sonneberg, Germany

Between 1871 and 1911, the firm of Johannes Franz manufactured and exported dressed dolls, automata, and jointed dolls. Franz's trademark is illustrated here; a semi-circular mark has been found on the company's automata. It includes the words **Gesetzlicher Schutz** in an arc; beneath run the words **Patent Amt № 5332.**

Frickmann & Lindner

(see Robert Carl)

Friedrichsrodaer Puppenfabrick

Friedrichsroda, Germany

Founded in 1922 as successor to Jäger & Co., Friedrichsrodaer registered **Brüderchen** (little brother) for ball-jointed dolls, bent-limb babies, and toddlers in 1923 and **Mamas Herzensschatzl** (mama's little darling) in 1927.

Fulper Pottery Co.

Flemington, New Jersey

A pottery firm founded in 1805, Fulper began to make bisque dolls' head in 1918 to compensate for the absence of German ones during the first World War. Using molds from Armand Marseille, Fulper produced heads under the guidance of the Horsman Company, for whom many of the heads were intended. Fulper also made all-bisque dolls, including **Kewpies** and the **Peterkin** doll designed by Helen Trowbridge. It ceased to manufacture dolls in 1920.

Otto Gans
Waltershausen and Finsterbergen,
Germany

Otto Gans founded his own doll firm after
leaving Gans & Seyfarth in 1922. He
manufactured voice mechanisms for dolls,
along with bisque dolls' heads, bathing
dolls, and walking dolls. Gans used the
trademarks **My Dearie** (1922) and **Oga**
(1925). The circular trademark **Kinder-
traum** (child's dream) was registered in
1930.

G
*Made in
Germany*

G
6789/26

Otto Gans
Germany
975
A. 5 M.

Gans & Seyfarth
Waltershausen, Germany

Founded in 1908 by Otto Gans and Hugo
Seyfarth, this doll factory specialized in doll
parts and jointed dolls. Among its trademarks were **Dolly Mine** (1911) and **Fine
Jointed Doll** (1910); in 1919 it advertised

Schalk (rascal) and **Racker** (rogue) as two
of its available dolls. The partners dissolved
the firm in 1922 and formed new ones
individually.

Germany
G.&S
3

Gans & Seyfarth.

J. Roger Gault
Paris

In 1917, Gault registered **Plastolite** as his
trademark for a plastic paste used for dolls
and dolls' heads.

PLASTOLITE

Gaultier
St. Maurice, Charenton, Seine, and
Paris

Between 1860 and at least 1916, the shop
of Gaultier manufactured porcelain dolls'
heads. Not all heads marked **F G** can be
determined to have been made by Gaultier,

F. 3. G

La Poupée de France

but one can discriminate to a certain de-
gree, since Gaultier dolls won several international competitions and must have
been of corresponding quality. Some
Gesland dolls have Gaultier heads.

Gerbaulet Frères
Paris

Registered Le "Coquet Bébé" as a
trademark in 1910, along with the initials
GF. In 1926, registered Bébé Olga.

Gem Toy Co.
New York City

Gem Toy Co., founded in 1913, produced
composition and soft-body dolls. It
registered Gem as a trademark in 1925.
Among its trade names were Baby's Voice,
Mother's Choice (1924), Excelsior (1920),
Flossie Featherweight (1922), Just Born
(1925), and O-U-Kids (1918).

Gerling Toy Co.
New York City, London, and
Neustadt, Germany

Arthur Gerling produced stuffed dolls and
composition dolls after 1912. He specialized in voices, gaining several patents for
reed- and bellows-operated devices. A doll
from c. 1925 bears his name as a mark.

Pat Pending
GERLING

German American Doll Co.
(see Regal Doll Manufacturing Co.)

Gesland
Paris

Beginning in 1860, Gesland made wire-
frame dolls with stockinet covering; the
firm probably used Gaultier porcelain
heads on some of its dolls (Gesland appears
on the bodies of such dolls). Gesland advertised a wide range of bébés in the early
1900s. J. Ortiz, the firm's owner after
Gesland, registered the trademark Excelsior Bébé in 1916.

BÉBÉ E. GESLAND
BTE. S.G.D.G.
5, RUE BERANGER. 5
PARIS

EXCELSIOR BÉBÉ

Carl Geyer & Co.
Sonneberg, Germany

Founded in 1882, Carl Geyer & Co.
manufactured stiff-jointed dolls and doll
accessories. Its four trademarks were
registered in 1885 (circular), 1900 (Bébé
Habille and the cornucopia), and 1902
(Liliput). Renamed Carl Geyer & Söhne

after the death of its founder in 1913, the company was in business until the early 1930s.

Giebeler-Falk Doll Corp.
New York City

Founded in 1918, the firm made wooden and aluminum dolls. In 1919 it registered **Gie-Fa** as a trademark for dolls and doll parts and advertised **Primadonna,** a phonograph doll with a turntable in its head on which small records could be played.

2 5

U.S. PAT.

Gie-Fa

Gimbel Bros.
New York City and Philadelphia

Several large doll manufacturers here and abroad supplied this department store with bisque dolls; around 1910 Gimbel employees dressed the dolls in costumes made on the premises. (Simon & Halbig dolls' heads made for the department store are marked with the store's name or a **G.**) Gimbels also sold Kewpie dolls supplied to them by Borgfeldt after 1914.

550

Germany

G

SIMON & HALBIG

S & H

Gimbel Bros.

Germany

Giotti
Nice, France

Registered **Magali** as a trademark for his felt art dolls in 1926.

F & W Goebel
Oeslau, Germany

In 1876 Franz Detleff Goebel and his son, William, built a porcelain factory (which they called Wilhelmsfeld) and were manufacturing porcelain dolls' heads by 1887. The company's heads were made for other German doll manufacturers, including Max Handwerck. William Goebel took over the business from his father in 1893, at which time the firm's name was changed to William Goebel. By 1908, Goebel was making baby dolls and bathing dolls in addition to heads. Among the mold numbers used were 30, 34, 46, 54, 60, 73, 77A, 77B, 80, 82, 83, 84, 85, 86A, 86B, 87, 88, 89, 90, 91, 92, 106, 107, 110, 111, 114, 120, 121, 122, 123, 124, 125, 126, 217, 283, 285, 286, 317, 319, 320, 321, 322, 330, 340, 350, and 501. With few exceptions, the triple-digit numbers were produced in the 1920s and early '30s; double-digit numbers were used earlier. Among the marks found on Goebel heads, the crown with entwined WG beneath was used no earlier than 1900.

Walter Goebel
Sonneberg, Germany

Registered **Muing** as a trademark in 1928.

Max Göhring
Oberlin, Germany

Produced character babies and jointed dolls c. 1920-1925; registered girl-in-swing trademark in 1924.

Eugene Goldberger
New York City

Registered **Miss Charming** as a trademark in 1936.

Edgard Goldstein & Co.
Berlin

Goldstein registered a trademark for dolls in 1919.

Charles Goodyear
New Haven, Connecticut

Rubber dolls made by this famous firm are marked **Goodyear** or **Goodyear's Pat. May 6, 1851. Ext 1865.** (The 1851 date reflects the date Nelson Goodyear, Charles's brother, patented his invention of hard rubber.)

Goss & Co.
Stoke-on-Trent, England

Primarily a manufacturer of porcelain busts during the 19th century, the company produced fine bisque heads during the first few decades of the 20th. Potteries Toy Co. assembled the dolls and Bawo & Dotter distributed them.

GOSS
30

Arthur Gotthelf
Remscheid, Germany

Gotthelf registered **Ulla-Puppe** as a trademark for his porcelain- and bisque-headed dolls in 1922.

Gove Manufacturing Co.
Williamsport, Pennsylvania

Helen N. Gove registered her trademark, **Uneke**, for dolls in 1928.

Grandjean
Paris

Used the trade name **Bébé Bijou** for jointed bébés. Between the years 1887 and 1889, over two million of these dolls were made.

–M–
PARIS
G D
4

Jane Gray Co.
New York City

Jane Gray (Stokes) designed and made dolls from 1915 to 1924. Among the trade names she advertised were **Jazz Hound** (1923), **Kuddles** (1917), and **Little Boy Blue** (1921). Her major achievement, however, was the design and manufacture of **Margaret Vale's Celebrity Creations,** a line of dolls depicting famous performers, which was launched in 1924. Margaret Vale, Woodrow Wilson's niece, selected the individuals to be depicted and secured the rights to make the dolls. Each wore a tag giving the name of the celebrity, the character he or she portrayed (costumes were carefully selected to imitate the movie or play involved), and a facsimile autograph. Among the celebrities and characters in the series were:

Ada May
Carroll McComas
Constance Binney
Constance Talmadge
Dorothy Stone
Edith Day
Emma Haig

Fred Stone
Glenn Hunter
Lady Diana Manners
Laurette Taylor
Lillian Gish
Mary Carroll
Mary Hay
Mary Nash
Mitzi
Ramon Navarro

Greif-Puppenkunst
Dresden, Germany

Manufactured stuffed felt and plush dolls
c. 1927; used Ernst Heubach heads.

Schlagwort des Betriebes
=ECHTE RASSE=
die wirklich weichgeftopfte
·SONDER KLASSE·
*
ERICH REISER, Dresden,
„GREIF TIERKUNST."

"Greif."
Puppenkunst
Germany
7/o

Greiner & Co.
Steinach, Germany

Founded as a trading company in 1860,
Greiner & Co. began making leather dolls
and doll parts in 1890. Many of its dolls,
with bisque heads by Armand Marseille,

Eichhorn, and Ernst Heubach, were sold
to Borgfeldt.

Ludwig Greiner
Philadelphia

Papier-mâché dolls' heads were made by
Greiner beginning in 1840; after 1874, the
firm was known as Greiner Brothers and
was then succeeded by Knell Brothers in
1890. It is not unusual to find Greiner
heads on bodies made by Jacob Lacmann,
also of Philadelphia.

GREINER'S
IMPROVED
PATENT HEADS
Pat. March 30th. '58.

John B. Gruelle
New York City and Norwalk,
Connecticut

Created the Raggedy Ann doll and
patented it in 1915. Early specimens of this
doll, looking little like their modern
counterparts, are marked **Patented Sept. 7,
1915** on the front of the torso.

Jean-Marie Guepratte
Paris

Jean-Marie Guepratte registered **Bébé-Soleil** as a trademark in 1891. The firm operated c. 1881-1898 and specialized in dolls' heads.

Mademoiselle Marthe Guerin
Paris

Registered her trademark for dolls in 1915.

François Guillard
Paris

Guillard was making and selling dolls by 1847. His successors managed the firm until 1867, when Rémond & Perreau succeeded them. The **Rémond** name and the name of his shop, **A La Galerie Vivienne**, have been found on a sticker dating from c. 1890.

Louis Guillet
Paris

Registered the trademark **Amour-Bèbé** in 1896.

AMOUR - BÉBÉ

Silas Guillon
Paris

Registered the trademark **Camelia** for art dolls and dolls' heads, 1926.

C. Erich Günther
Dresden, Germany

Made unbreakable art dolls, 1922.

Gutmann & Schiffnie
Nuremberg and Sonneberg, Germany

Founded around 1900, Gutmann & Schiffnie manufactured and sold dolls. Among the trade names it registered were **Bébé l'Avenir** (1907), **Bébé Coiffure** (1911), **Boy Scouts** (1914), **Eclaireur** (1914), **Guschi** (1922), and **Mona Lisa** (1914).

guschi Germany   *G&$*

Bébé l'Avenir

"BÉBÉ-COIFFURE"

'Bébé l'Avenir'

"MONA LISA"

H

Gebrüder Haag
Sonneberg, Germany

Founded in 1878, Gebrüder Haag sold dolls and dolls' heads. Its first trademark, **Biskuit-Imitation**, was registered in 1886; its second was used after 1920.

Haas & Czjzek
(see Lippert & Haas)

Hermann Hachmeister
Sonneberg, Germany

Founded in 1872 as Hachmeister & Franz, this factory manufactured nanking and porcelain dolls and composition heads. Its trademark was registered in 1880; in 1920, under new management, it became known as Hachmeister & Co.

Hahn & Co.
Nuremburg, Germany

Hahn & Co. registered **Hanco** as a trademark for dolls, cloth animals, and plush bears in 1921.

Hamburger & Co.
New York City, Berlin, and Nuremburg

Founded in 1889, this American company supplied dolls to Strawbridge & Clothier and other American stores. It produced several lines of dolls and registered many patents for dressed and jointed dolls. Its trademarks, **D.P.** and **H & C**, were registered in 1895. Among the trade names Hamburger used were **Brownie Policeman** (1905), **Dolly Dimple** (1907), **Imperial** (1898), **Imperial H & Co.** (1901), **Marguerite** (1903), **Old Glory** (1902), **Lillian Russell** (1903), **Santa** (1901), and **Viola** (1903). Hamburger used heads made by other German companies, among them Gebrüder Heubach (Dolly Dimple) and Simon & Halbig (Imperial and Santa). Santa heads may be marked with just the trade name, with the name and mold number 1249 or 1429, or just with the mold number. The firm closed in 1909.

S&H 1249 DEP.
Germany
12
SANTA

Made in Germany
Viola
H.&Co.

𝕯.𝕻. H.&-C.
Registered.

5777
DEP
DOLLY DIMPLE
H
Germany
7

Hamley Bros.
London

During the second half of the 19th century and the early years of the 20th, Hamley Bros. imported dolls from Europe and America, including Pierotti dolls, and exported dolls all over the world. Its name is found on labels attached to dolls; among the trademarks it registered were:

The Bluestocking Dolls (1917)
Buster Brown (1904)
Cilly Billy (1919)
Diddums (1920)
Elfie (1913)
Fumsup (1914—see mark)
Lulu (1916)
Ni-Ni (1911)
Pooksie (1914)
Thumbs Up (1914—see mark)
Wu Wu (1915)

FUMS UP
THUMBS UP

S. Hancock & Sons
Cauldon, England

Founded in 1891, Hancock produced some of the finest English porcelain dolls' heads, most with intaglio eyes. By 1935, the firm had merged with Corona Pottery, Hanley. Marks found on Hancock dolls include **S.H. & S., N.T.I.** (on bodies), and **Made in England. H. & S.P. Hancock.**

NTI BOY
ENGLISH MAKE

Heinrich Handwerck
Waltershausen, Germany

Heinrich Handwerck founded his company in 1886 and produced a variety of ball-jointed dolls, many with heads of his own design which were made at the Simon & Halbig factory, including Bébé Superior (mold number 174). After his death in 1902, Kämmer & Reinhardt bought the factory, although it kept the Handwerck name. Under its new management, Handwerck manufactured character dolls and babies and doll parts. The firm closed in 1918, but reopened in 1921 under the ownership of Heinrich Handwerck, Jr., who moved the facilities to Gotha, where he manufactured ball-jointed dolls until the company's closing in 1932.

Mold numbers 69, 79, 89, 99, 109, 119, 139, 174, 189, and 199 have been found on Handwerck dolls. In addition, variants of the initials (**H, HHW, HchH,** etc.) were used. Among the trade names introduced by the company were **Baby Cut** (1914), **Bébé Cosmopolite** (1895), **Bébé de Réclame** (1898), **Bébé Superior** (1913), **La Belle** (1914), **La Bonita** (1914), and **Lotti** (1914).

Heinrich Handwerck
Germany

7

Heinrich Handwerck
D.R.Patent No 100279
Germany

139.295.

H̄

Hch2H

Hch 6/0H
Germany

Germany
HANDWERCK
HALBIG

HH
420
Germany
72

Germany
HH
S&H
4/0

79.3X
HW

Max Handwerck
Waltershausen, Germany

Founded in 1899, the Max Handwerck firm used dolls' heads from the factory of F & W Goebel and produced porcelain and bisque dolls, doll parts, and doll clothes. Trademarks registered include **Bébé Elite**

(1901), **Cornouloid-Doll Madame Butterfly** (1913), and **Triumph-Bébés** (1902). The firm was operative through the 1920s.

Dep.
Elite
E%

Germany
MAX
HANDWERCK
0¼

Max Handwerk
Bebe Elite
B90/185
4½
Germany

Hannebelle
Paris

Made bisque dolls, beginning in 1909.

Depose
AH
PARIS

Harburger Gummiwarenfabrik
Harburg, Germany

Manufactured rubber wares, including rubber dolls called **Phoenix Gummipuppen**, c. 1925. Its trademark was **Phoenix Quick.**

Carl Harmus Jr.
Sonneberg, Germany

Founded in 1887, the firm manufactured jointed dolls and dolls' heads. Between 1900 and the 1920s, it specialized in drinking and speaking dolls and stuffed animals.

Harmus
2

Carl Hartmann
Neustadt, Germany

Founded in 1899, Hartmann produced bisque-headed dolls with jointed bodies and, later, character babies and dolls. As an exporter, the company advertised dolls by Kämmer & Reinhardt and often supplied unmarked dolls to its customers on request. Among the trade names Hartmann used were Erika (1922), Globe-Baby (1899), Hansa (1902), Paladin-Baby (1903), and Thuringia (1902). The company operated into the 1930s.

Globe Baby
DEP
Germany
C₃H

DEP
CH
10%
GERMANY

Karl Hartmann
Stockheim, Germany

Between 1911 and 1926, Hartmann manufactured ball-jointed dolls and character bent-limb babies with papier-mâché heads.

Hausman & Zatulove
New York City

Makers of Ku-Tee cloth dolls with jointed limbs; its trademark, Hau-zat (1919), was a clever amalgam of the names of the firm's two owners.

Paul Hausmeister & Co.
Göppingen, Germany

In 1909 the firm registered a stork as a trademark for its gelatin-based dolls' heads. Note its similarity to the mark of the Parsons-Jackson Company, which made a celluloid-type doll.

George H. Hawkins
New York City

Hawkins obtained a patent in 1868 for making dolls' head by molding glue-saturated cloth. His shoulder heads are found on some mechanical and tricycle-riding dolls and bear the mark X.L.C.R., representing his brand name, Excelsior.

Hawkins & Stubblefield

Rogers, Arkansas

Registered **SAM-ME** as a trademark for dolls in 1917.

"SAM-ME"

Heber & Co.

Neustadt, Germany

The firm, which operated from 1900 to 1922, produced porcelain dolls' heads.

 514 c 16/0

Else L. Hecht

Munich

Founded in 1913; created art dolls. In 1926, the firm was renamed Else Lill Kolmar-Hecht.

Therese Heininger

Dresden, Germany

Registered **Original Rose Hein Puppen** as a trademark in 1925.

Rudolph Heinz & Co.

Neuhaus am Rennweg, Germany

This porcelain factory was founded in 1858; little of its production was devoted to dolls until the 1920s, when the company name had been changed to Aelteste Volkstedter Porzellanfabrik AG (thus the initials **AV** on the mark).

9500
Neuhaus
AV.
am Rug.
2/0 ˣ
Germany

Berthold Helk

Neustadt, Germany

Helk manufactured cloth dolls and doll bodies, c. 1913-1930. He used two trademarks, **Rinaldo** and **Torino**, to signify the difference in quality between the two types of dolls he produced, inexpensive and expensive respectively. The mark **Beha** is the phonetic equivalent of the initials "B" and "H" in German.

Adolf Heller

Waltershausen, Germany

Heller founded his own company in 1909, after several years in partnership with Hugo Seyfarth. He manufactured ball-jointed dolls and talking character babies under two trade names, **Meine Goldperle** (1914) and **Mein Liebes Kind** (1925).

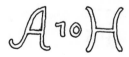

Alfred Heller
Meiningen, Germany

Made metal dolls' heads under the trade name **Diana** (1903) for the first decade of the 20th century.

D. R. G. M. 160638

 Made in Germany

Viktoria

J. H.

15/0

Henze & Steinhäuser
Erfurt and Gehren, Germany

Founded in 1869, the company originally produced dolls in handmade national costumes. In 1886, the firm moved to Gehren, where it manufactured woolen dolls by machine. After an interruption of some years, business began again c. 1903 and continued until c. 1930, with a variety of dressed dolls which were offered with woolen or celluloid heads. Trademarks which the firm registered were **Gehrenia** (1912) and **Henza** (1925).

Hering & Sohn
Köppelsdorf, Germany

This firm, from its establishment in 1893, passed through several owners before it stopped producing bisque dolls' heads in 1912. Most heads were manufactured under the direction of Julius Hering after 1902; those are marked **J.H. & W., J.H.S.,** or **J.H. & S.**

Hermsdorfer Celluloidwarenfabrik
Berlin-Hermsdorf

Between 1923 and 1926, the firm advertised celluloid dolls, some of which drank from an attached bottle. One of the company's trademarks was **Marienkafer** (lady bug).

E.J. Herte
Milwaukee, Wisconsin

Registered **Billie the Brownie** as a trademark for dolls in 1937.

Hertel, Schwab, & Co.
Stutzhaus, Germany

Founded in 1910, the Stutzhaus porcelain factory manufactured bisque dolls' heads, character dolls, and bathing dolls for at least two decades. The Ciesliks point out that many of the firm's character baby mold numbers (150, 163, 165, 173) have been attributed to Kestner, but were, in fact, manufactured by Hertel, Schwab. The company produced many of its heads for other German manufacturers such as Kley & Hahn and Koenig & Wernicke; some of the molds (such as **Bye-Lo**) were intended for the American market, where Borgfeldt and Louis Wolf were among Hertel, Schwab's major distributors. Strobel & Wilken ordered its **Jubilee** line of googly-eyed dolls from the firm soon after it was established. They bore mold numbers 163, 165, 172, and 173.

Mold numbers that are known to have been produced by the company include 130, 132, 133, 134, 135, 136, 138, 141, 142, 143, 147, 148, 149, 150, 151, 152, 157, 158, 159, 160, 161, 162, 163, 165, 166, 167, 169, 170, 172, 173, 176, 180, 200, 208, 217, 220, and 222.

152
L.W. & Co
12

Made in Germany
151/0

Hertwig & Co.
Katzhütte, Germany

The porcelain and earthenware factory was founded in 1864 and was manufacturing porcelain dolls' heads within twenty years. The firm produced nanking dolls along with a variety of others. Trademarks registered were **Hewika** (1925) and **Biscoloid** (1929). Hertwig & Co. manufactured **Pet Name** dolls' heads for Butler Brothers, New York. Hertwig also produced **Buster Brown** dolls in the 1920s and was in operation until at least the beginning of World War II.

Herzpuppen-Fabrik
Berlin

Registered **H.P.F.** as a trademark in 1923 for wax dolls' heads and art and tea-cozy dolls.

Albin Hess
Schalkau, Germany

Hess founded his company in 1913, producing doll accessories. By 1922, he manufactured dressed dolls, dolls with moving eyes, and dolls with music boxes included. In 1930, he registered the trademark **Gymnastik-Doll.**

Ernst Heubach
Köppelsdorf, Germany

Ernst Heubach founded a porcelain factory in 1887 for the manufacture of bisque dolls' heads and bathing dolls. After 1910, he specialized in character dolls, including exotic representations of blacks, and produced heads for other German makers, including A. Wislizenus, Gebrüder Ohlhaver, Cuno & Otto Dressel, and Luge & Co. In 1919, Heubach merged his firm with that of Armand Marseille; the new partnership was called United Porcelain Factory of Köppelsdorf. The use of the trade name **Heubach Köppelsdorf** as part of the mark is generally felt to date a doll as having been made after the merger. The partnership ended in 1932.

Among the mold numbers attributed to Ernst Heubach are 219, 235, 236, 237,

238, 241, 242, 250, 251, 252, 259, 260, 261, 262, 263, 264, 266, 267, 268, 269, 271, 274, 275, 276, 281, 282, 283, 284, 289, 291, 292, 300, 301, 302, 312, 313, 317, 320, 321, 323, 334, 339, 340, 341, 342, 343, 344, 345, 348, 349, 350, 399, 400, 406, 407, 414, 418, 427, 437, 438, 439, 444, 445, 448, 450, 451, 452, 458, 459, 463, 471, and 480. Early shoulder heads are marked with a horseshoe and the year of manufacture.

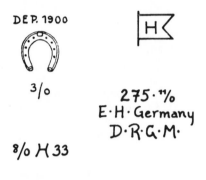

DE P. 1900

3/0

8/0 H 33

275·¹⁷/₀
E·H·Germany
D·R·G·M·

Heubach· Köppessdorf
339·³/₀
Germany

Gebrüder Heubach
Lichte, Germany

The Heubach family bought a Lichte porcelain factory in 1840 and began to produce porcelain figurines shortly thereafter. Its rising sun trademark was registered in 1882, although Heubach is not known to have made its famous porcelain dolls' heads with intaglio eyes until around 1910, when the square **Heubach** trademark was first registered. Because the factory manufactured such an enormous quantity and range of character dolls' heads and all-bisque dolls, positive identification is difficult. Some of the company's marks are illustrated here. Far too numerous to list are the hundreds of mold numbers that appeared in series from the 5600s to the 12,000s. Many of the firm's heads were made for other German companies as well as for ex-

port to the United States. One of its most appealing and popular character dolls, **Whistling Jim,** was made for Wagner & Zetsche of Ilmenau.

77 ℗ 45
Germany

8192
Germany
Gebrüder Heubach

Ⓖ   H

6969
8
Germany

8192
Germany.
Sebrüder Heubach

4½

G·OH.

Heubach, Kämpfe & Sontag
Wallendorf, Germany

A porcelain factory built in 1763, it produced dolls' heads between 1874 and 1894.

Carl Heumann
Sonneberg, Germany

Founded in 1902, this firm operated until at least 1930. Its most famous doll, **Suck-Thumb Baby**, was produced in the late 1920s.

Hewitt Bros.
Longton, England

Manufactured porcelain dolls. Registered the trademark **Suner** in 1920 and also used the mark **H & L**.

H & L
WILLOW②ENGLAND

Hermann Heyde
Dresden, Germany

Founded in 1867; registered its trademark for dolls and doll outfits in 1910. Continued operation until at least 1920.

Edmond Hieulle
Paris

Registered **Parfait-Bébé** and **Montreuil-Bébé** as trademarks in 1917, along with a coat of arms bearing the initials **MSB**.

PARFAIT-BÉBÉ
PARIS

MONTREUIL-BÉBÉ

Thomas H. Hindle, Jr.
New York City

Hindle manufactured a cherubic doll and registered **Wot-Zat** as a trademark in 1915.

Hinrichs & Co.
New York City

Made and imported dressed dolls, china dolls, rubber dolls, jointed dolls, and dolls' heads, 1890-1904. Registered **H & Co.** as a trademark and was known to deal extensively with Germany's Heinrich Handwerck.

H & Cº

Fernand and Paul Hirschler
Paris

Registered a trademark, **Le Jouet Artistique** (1919), for dolls; used the initials **F.P.H.** as well.

Hitz, Jacobs & Kassler
New York City

A doll importer, Hitz, Jacobs & Kassler was founded in 1918. It sold the **Kiddiejoy** line (heads by Armand Marseille), **Hoopla Girls**, and **Ja Ja** dolls. In 1925, the firm became known as Jacobs & Kassler.

HJK   JK

Carl Horn Nachf.

Dresden, Germany

Manufactured miniature dolls and dolls dressed in national costumes, c. 1916-1930.

E. I. Horsman & Co.

New York City

During the 1870s, Edward I. Horsman, a toy distributor, began to import dolls from Europe. By 1900, his firm was manufacturing dolls as well and early on showed a penchant for exploiting the latest American fads and trends. When rag dolls became popular, Horsman produced a line with photographic faces (1907). International events such as Cook's and Peary's North Pole expedition (1909) were recognized, as was the outbreak of World War I. Horsman employed notable artists to design its dolls; among them were Charles Twelvetrees, Grace Drayton, Helen Trowbridge, and Laura Gardin. In 1909, Horsman secured exclusive production of the Aetna Company's **Can't Break 'Em** heads; less than ten years later (1918), the two companies merged, producing a new composition material called **Adtocolite**. In addition, Horsman worked with Fulper Pottery to produce American bisque heads. After 1925, rights to the Horsman name were purchased by Regal Doll Manufacturing Company, which uses it to this day. Among the trade names the company registered were:

Annette (1912)
Army Nurse (1917)
Art Dolls (1910)
Baby Bill (1911)
Baby Blossom (1913)
Baby Bobby (1911)
Baby Bumps (1910—see mark)
Baby Darling (1915)
Baby Butterfly (1913)
Baby Horsman (1923)
Baby Peterkin (1911)

Baby Rosebud (1914)
Babyland Rag (1904)
Bauernkinder (1914)
Bébé Premier (1911)
Betty (1909)
Betty Blazer (1912)
Betty Bright (1916)
Big Baby Bumps (1910)
Big Candy Kid (1911)
Big Sister (1916)
Billiken (1909)
Billy Blink (1912)
Bingo (1911)
Blink (1915)
Blue Bird Doll (1920)
Bo Peep (1909)
Bobby (1910)
Bobby Bright (1906)
Boy Scout (1913)
Bright Star (1930s)
British Tommy (1917)
Bye Bye Kiddies (1917)
Camp Fire Girl (1913)
Campbell Kids (1910)
The Candy Kid (1911)
Canton Kids (1915)
Carl (1911)
Carnival Baby (1912)
Chinkee (1911)
Christening Baby (1913)
The Colgate Kid (1914)
Cotton Joe (1911)
Cy (1909)
Cycle Kids (1915)
Daisy Darling (1906)
Daisy Dimple (1912)
Drowsy Dick (1914)
Dutch Hans, Dutch Gretchen (1911)
Eric (1913)
Fairy (1911)
Gee-Gee Dolly (1912)
Gene Carr Kids (1916)
Gold Medal Prize Baby (1911)
Golden Jubilee (1915)
Golf Boy, Golf Girl (1909)
Happy Hiram (1912)
HEbees-SHEbees (1925)
Helen (1914)
Hitchy Koo (1913)
Jack Tar (1911)
Jackie Coogan Kid (1921)
Jane (1915)
Janet (1911)

Jap Rose Kids (1911)
Joffre (1918)
Kickapoo (1911)
Life Like Faces (1906)
Little Billy (1912)
Little Fairy (1906)
Litle Mary Mix-Up (1919)
Little Peterkin (1918)
Little San Toy (1911)
Little Sunshine (1913)
Manikin Dolls (1920)
Mascot (1912)
Master Sam (1917)
Merry Max (1913)
Middie (1917)
Mike (1915)
Mischievous Pippen (1910)
Miss Campbell (1914)
Miss Janet (1914)
Miss Mischief (1911)
Miss Sam (1917)
Nancy Lee (1912)
Nature Babies (1912)
Our Baby (1913)
The Panama Kid (1915)
Patty-Cake (1918)
Peasant Children (1917)
Peek-a-Boo (1913)
Peter Pan (1913)
Peterkin (1910)
Phoebe (1914)
Pinafore (1920)
Pocahontas (1911)
Polly (1914)
Polly Prue (1912)
Polly Wise (1921)
Pop Eyes (1916)
Robbie Reefer (1912)
Rookie (1917)
Rosebud Babies (1920)
School Boy, School Girl (1911)
Skinney (1915)
Snookums (1910)
Snowball (1915)
Stella (1903)
Sucker Thumb (1912)
Sunbonnet Girl (1911)
Sunbonnet Sal (1912)
Sunbonnet Sue (1909)
Sunshine (1913)
Teddy (1911)
Tom Thumb (1911)
Tommy Trim (1906)

Toodles (1911)
Tootsie (1911)
Topsy (1909)
Tynie Baby (1924)
Uncle Sam's Kids (1917)

H.C.Q.   ©
1916   E.I.H. CO. INC.

© 1924

E.I. HORSMAN INC.
Made in
Germany

Arthur E. Hotchkiss
New Haven, Connecticut

Created the walking Empress Eugenie Doll (1875), which contained a clockwork mechanism; the patent date, **September 21, 1875**, was incised on each shoe.

Adolf Hülss
Waltershausen, Germany

In operation by 1913, the firm of Adolf Hülss produced various jointed dolls, bent-limb babies, bisque heads, and doll parts. The **AHW** trademark was registered in 1925, **Nesthakchen** in 1927. Hülss also used Simon & Halbig heads, according to the mark shown here, including mold numbers 156 and 157, and was known to use celluloid heads by Rheinische Gummi as well.

SIMON & HALBIG

Made in Germany 156/11

Dr. Paul Hunaeus
Hannover-Linden, Germany

Founded in 1890, the Hunaeus factory produced celluloid dolls and dolls' heads. Its **PH** trademark was registered in 1901, **Natura** in 1927, and **Peha** in 1928. Hunaeus merged with Rheinische Gummi- und Celluloid-Fabrik in 1930.

Maison Huret
Paris

Produced a variety of dolls from c. 1850 to at least 1920; a variation of one of the marks shown was generally stamped on the chest.

MÉDAILLE D'ARGENT
HURET
22 Boulev.d Montmartre
PARIS
EXP ON UNIVER.LLE 1867

HURET

68 RUE DE LA BOETIE

Huttinger & Buschor
Behringerdorf, Germany

Founded in 1920, Huttinger & Buschor registered its **Casadora** trademark in the following year. The name designated both bent-limb babies and jointed dolls, all designed to mimic a number of life-like movements, including crying, head-shaking, walking, and hand-clapping. The company continued in operation throughout the 1920s.

Ideal Novelty & Toy Co.
Brooklyn, New York

Morris Michtom founded his successful company c. 1906 and by 1909 was manufacturing unbreakable character dolls; the firm boasted that the durability of its composition material was unequaled. Ideal made hundreds of types of dolls, many of which could walk and had sleeping eyes. Most are easily identifiable, since the **Ideal** name has always been incorporated in the marks used through the years. One of Ideal's more successful dolls during the 1930s was **Shirley Temple.** The company continues to make dolls today; among the trade names introduced before World War II are:

Admiral Dot (1914)
Arctic Boy (1913)
Baby Bettie (1913)
Baby Betty (1917)
Baby Bi-Face (1916)
Baby Bunting (1914)
Baby Lolo (1914)
Baby Marion (1913)
Baby Mine (1911)
Baby Paula (1914)
Baby Snooks (1938)
Baby Talc (1915)
Baseball Kids (1915)
Beau Brummel (1924)
Betsy Wetsy (1937)
Broncho Bill (1914)
Bulgarian Princess (1914)
Captain Jinks (1912)
Carrie Joy (1924)
Clown with Box of Cookies (Zu-Zu Kid) (1916)
Columbia Kids (1917)
Compo Baby (1917)
Country Cousins (1913)
Cracker Jack Boy (1917)
Dandy Kid (1911)
Dolly Varden (1915)
Dorothy (c. 1939)
Dottie Dimples (1915)
Deanna Durbin (1938)
Elsie (1918)
Farmer Kids (1915)
Flora (1913)
Flossie Flirt (1924)
Freddie (1913)
Gabby (1939)
Greenwich Village Vincent, Vivian (1923)
Hush-a-Bye-Baby (1925)
Jenny Wren (1915)
Jiminy Cricket (1940)

Liberty Boy (1917)
Little Mother Teaching Dolly to Walk (1920)
Little Princess (1914)
Mabel (1916)
Magic Skin Baby (1940)
The Middy Girl (1913)
Miss Rainshine (1922)
Mortimer Snerd (1938)
Nancy Jane (1922)
Naughty Marietta (1912)
Old Glory Kids (1916)
Our Pet (1915)
Papa and Mama Dolls (1922)
Peter Pan (1928)
Pinocchio (1940)
Poppa-Momma Doll (1922)
Prize Baby (1915)
Rosy (Miss Rosy Cheeks) (1925)
Russian Boy (1912)
Sanitary Baby (1915)
Shirley Temple (1930s—see mark)
Sleeping Beauty (1917)
Snoozie (1933)
Soozie Smiles (1923)
Snow White and the Seven Dwarfs (1939)
Sucker Thumb Baby (1924)
Sunny Jim (1914)
Surprise Baby (1923)
Sweater Boy (1917)
Tennis Girl (1915)
Ticklette (1931)
Tiny Toddler (1913)
Uneeda Biscuit Boy (Uneeda Kid) (1915)
Walking, Talking, Sleeping (1920s)
Zu-Zu Kid (1916)

Trade Mark

Carl A. Illing & Co.

Sonneberg, Germany

Founded in 1925, the firm was called the Illco Doll Factory by 1930.

Indestructo Specialties Co.

New York City

Registered ISCO as a trademark for unbreakable character dolls in 1915; also used Sunshine Kids as a trademark in the same year.

India Rubber Comb Co.

New York City

Produced rubber dolls after 1850, using the Goodyear patent.

I.R. COMB Co.

Abraham and Henry Isaacs

London

Sold the Cherub Doll (1886) among other rag dolls and imported dressed dolls.

J

Jacobs & Kassler

(see Hitz, Jacobs & Kassler)

Jäger & Co.

(see Friedrichsrodaer Puppenfabrik)

Jointed Doll Co.

North Springfield, Vermont

Made wooden jointed dolls and composition dolls' heads. A black paper band is sometimes found around the waist of these dolls, which reads Improved Jointed Doll, pat. April 29 '79, Dec. 7 '80, & Nov. 7 '82.

E. S. Judge & Co.

Baltimore and Philadelphia

Edward S. Judge registered two patents—

one in 1868 for the improvement of papier-mâché and another in 1875 for papier-mâché heads. His marks generally include a patent date, either the one illustrated or Judge's Indestructible Doll Head, No. 3, March 24th, 1868. When E. S. Judge & Co. became Judge & Early is not known.

Walter Jügelt

Neustadt, Germany

Manufactured dressed dolls, 1923-1924.

Jullien

Paris

Founded in 1863, the Jullien firm first produced novelties; after 1875 records confirm that several types of dolls, including nanking and wooden dolls and musical figures, or marottes, were also offered. Jullien introduced L'Universal (1892) as a trade name for a composition bébé.

JuLLieN

Jumeau

Paris

The Jumeau establishment (Maison Jumeau), the recipient of many awards at the major 19th-century trade fairs, began manufacturing dolls when Pierre Francois Jumeau, in a partnership called Belton & Jumeau, established a doll factory in 1843. Although the death of Belton brought the partnership to an end, the dolls that Belton & Jumeau produced were highly regarded. Once Jumeau opened his own factory in Montreuil in 1873, Jumeau dolls were in demand for export because of their exquisite clothing. By this time, Jumeau heads were enjoying a reputation for fine painting and delicate shading, but Jumeau bodies were considered disappointingly crude. Émile Jumeau, Jumeau's eldest son, changed all this by establishing a factory that could handle all stages of production, including clothing. The result was the world-famous Jumeau facial expression, with its bewitching paperweight eyes. Jumeau received the gold medal at the 1878 Paris Exposition; many dolls manufactured after that time bear the **Medaille d'Or** mark

or **MED. OR** 1878 on their bodies and shoes, respectively. By 1894, Émile Jumeau was called "Roi des Poupées" (the Doll King) and his dolls were in demand worldwide. In 1899, however, under intense economic pressure and in the face of growing German competition, Jumeau became a participating member of the S.F.B.J. syndicate. The company's name survived, and its **bee mark**, introduced in 1891 (as a stamp on the shoe sole), was also used by S.F.B.J. after 1921.

Exact identification of Jumeau dolls can be troublesome for a collector. Early Jumeau dolls do not bear marks; those with the initial J were made before Émile Jumeau became the firm's director (c. 1875), and it is difficult to authenticate its use beyond any doubt. In 1881, Émile Jumeau claimed that every doll he made had his name (or his initials) on it, but, when he drastically increased production in 1892, he eliminated the marks in many cases.

Among the marks attributed to Jumeau, the collector should be aware that the digits (from 6 to 14) which often appear on dolls' heads refer to size, not mold number. It is probable that Simon & Halbig reserved its mold numbers in the 200 series for Jumeau during the late 1880s, though no specific numbers have been identified. Among the trade names Jumeau used were **Bébé Français** (1896), **Bébé Incassable** (1885), **Bébé Jumeau** (1886), **Bébé Marcheur** (1895), **Bébé Phonographe** (1895), **Bébé Prodige** (1886), and **Parisiennes** (1885).

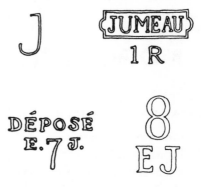

DÉPOSÉ
TETE JUMEAU
Bᵗᵉ SGDG
8

BÉBÉ JUMEAU
Bᵀᴱ S.G.D.G. DÉPOSÉ

Jacob Jung

Mannheim, Germany

In 1912, registered a trademark for celluloid dolls.

K

Lucien Kahn

Montreuil-sous-Bois, France

Registered **Moglette** as a trademark for dolls, 1926.

MOGLETTE

Joseph Kallus

(see Cameo Doll Co.)

Kämmer & Reinhardt

Waltershausen, Germany

This famous partnership, with Kämmer serving as the modeler and Reinhardt handling the business affairs, came into being in 1886 and established its lasting fame by introducing a famous line of character dolls (**charakterpuppe**) in 1909, of which **Baby** (mold number 100) is perhaps the best known. The K & R character dolls were a great success and are eagerly sought by collectors today, especially those with sulky expressions called "pouties." All K & R dolls after 1902 feature Simon & Halbig heads, but it is a mistake to think of these as S & H dolls since they were made to exact specifications from the K & R models. Many collectors continue to think that K & R dolls are actually S & H dolls because the K & R portion of the double mark is often obscured by the wig. (Kämmer & Reinhardt purchased Simon & Halbig in 1920, though the firms continued to operate independently.)

Kämmer & Reinhardt was an innovative company that not only pioneered in the development of character dolls, unusual eye mechanisms, and other lifelike features (such as teeth), but affected changes in doll anatomy to accommodate changing fashions in clothes, as well as to make the dolls appear more like real babies. The company is thought to have introduced the bent-limbed baby body in 1909, and in the 1920s, when little girls' dresses became quite short (and exposed ball-jointed knees appeared ugly in consequence), K & R was shrewd enough to introduce a doll with long lower legs that allowed the joint to occur above the knee.

Prior to its collaboration with Simon & Halbig in 1902, Kämmer & Reinhardt used few marks that have been definitely identified; two such are **K & R 192** and, simply, **K & R** (registered in 1896). Mold numbers attributed to the firm after 1902 include 100, 101, 102, 103, 104, 105, 106, 107, 108, 109, 110, 111, 112, 113, 114, 115, 115A, 116, 116A, 117, 117A, 117X, 117n, 118, 118A, 119, 120, 121, 122, 123, 125, 126, 127, 127n, 128, 129, 130, 131, 132, 133, 144, 146 through 169 inclusive, 170, 171, 173, 175, 200, 201, 210, 214, 225, 245, 246, 248, 255, 256, 265, 400, 401, 402, 403, 406, 500, 509, 510, 511, 526, 531, 550, 552, 600, 615, 626, 631, 651, 652, 665, 675, 700, 701, 715, 716, 717, 718, 719, 720, 721, 726, 727, 728, 730, 773, 775, 776, 777, 800, 817, 826, 828, 831, 873, 900, 901, 917, 921, 926, 952, 973, 975, and 977. Edmund Steiner's **Majestic** doll was registered by Kämmer & Reinhardt in 1902, although Armand Marseille's mark has been found on the head. Among the trade names registered by K & R were:

Baby (1909)
Baby Bauz (1911—produced for Käthe Kruse)
Charakterpuppe (1909)
Die Kokette (1907)
Der Schelm (1908)

Der Unart (1916)
The Flirt (1908)
Gretel (1909)
Hans (1909)
Majestic Doll (1902)
Mammy (1924)
Mein Kleines (1911)
Mein Liebling (My Darling) (produced from 1902 until at least the late '20s) (1902)
Mein Lieblingsbaby (1924)
My Sweet Darling (1912)
Nolli-Polli (1930)

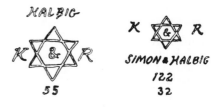

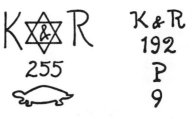

Louise R. Kampes
Atlantic City, New Jersey

Kamkins, Kampes's art dolls, were made of heavy cloth treated with rubber in a process she patented in 1920.

KAMKINS
A DOLLY MADE TO LOVE
PATENTED BY L.R.KAMPES
ATLANTIC CITY, N.J.

KAMKINS
A DOLLY MADE TO LOVE
.PATENTED.
FROM
L.R.KAMPES
STUDIOS
ATLANTIC CITY
N.J.

Marion Kaulitz
Gmund on Tegernsee, Germany

Produced art dolls in her workshop, c. 1908-1920; registered as trademarks Münchner Künstler Kaulitz-Puppen (1909) and Kaulitz (1911).

V2

Kaybee Doll & Toy Co.
Los Angeles

Registered Kaybee as a trademark (1918) for sleeping-eyed dolls and character dolls.

Keramisches Werke
Gräfenhain, Germany

Sculptors from the Simon & Halbig fac-

tory formed this ceramic workshop in the 1930s and produced papier-mâché dolls' heads during the early 1940s.

KW
G

134
12/0

K.W.
G.

136
12

J. D. Kestner
Waltershausen, Germany

Johann Daniel Kestner established a papier mâché factory in 1816 and was making wooden doll joints soon thereafter; he increased production steadily until his death in 1858. Five years later his grandson, Adolf, took control and within a decade was producing a wide variety of bisque, porcelain, wood, nanking, and composition dolls, as well as doll parts. In addition to manufacturing dolls of its own, Kestner worked with a number of other German and American firms. Leather bodies produced for Butler Brothers beginning in 1899 bear the JDK Germany trademark with crown, as well as the name Marvel within a rectangle (the first crown trademark had been registered in 1896). Walküre was produced for Kley & Hahn beginning in 1903; all-bisque Kewpies for Borgfeldt after 1914; character dolls for Catterfelder Puppenfabrik (marked Kestner & Comp. Porzellanfabrik) after World War I; and Bye-Lo heads and all-bisque Bye-Los for Butler Brothers starting in 1925. The popularity of the "million-dollar baby," as the Bye-Lo became known, led to many imitations: Kestner also made newborn lookalikes for Century Doll Company during the same period. After 1900, the company also made celluloid dolls and used the celluloid of Rheinische Gummi, but with its own special molds marked J.D.K., along with the Rheinische Gummi turtle mark.

Kestner's first trademark, a doll flanked

by two shoulder-heads, all within a circle, was registered in 1889. Dolls named **Excelsior** and **Bette** followed in 1893. **Hilda,** a very popular character doll, was first made in 1914. In 1897, Kestner registered its famous "alphabet" to denote sizes. Many Kestner heads are marked with one of the following letter/number series: B/6, C/7, D/8, E/9, F/10, G/11, H/12, J/13, K/14, L/15, M/16, or N/17. (The company also used fractions of the numeral in combination with the letters—e.g., K½/14½—to suggest even smaller differentiation in size.) Beginning in 1892, many Kestner dolls were marked **Made in Germany**; the famous **Crown Doll** trademark was first used in 1915.

Some Kestner character dolls made in the first two decades of the 20th century were marked only with the mold number. Such numbers include: 120, 121, 122 through 148 inclusive, 151, 152, 154, 155, 156, 159, 161, 162, 164, 166, 167, 168, 170, 171, 172, 174, 178 through 187 inclusive, 189, 190, 192, 195, 196, 199, 200, 201, 205 through 212 inclusive, 214, 215, 216, 218, 219, 220, 221, 234, 235, 236, 237, 239, 241, 242, 243, 245, 246, 247, 249, 250, 254, 255, 257, 260, 262, 263, 264, 270, 272, 279, 281, 282, and 292.

In addition, Kestner's all-bisque dolls (generally quite small ones) had their own mold numbers: 111, 122, 130, 141, 150, 179, 182, 184, 185, 186a, 186b, 187a, 187b, 189, 192, 195, 196, 198, 200, 208, 217, 500, 502, 504, 505, 511, 512, 514, 516, 517, 518, 519, 520, 522, 523, 524, 525, 526, 527, 528a, 531, 532, 533, 533a, 534, 535b, 537, 538 through 551 inclusive, 553, 554, 555, 556, 557, 559, 560, 561, 563, 565, 566, 567, 568, 570, 571, 572, 573, 574, 575, 577, 579, 586, 588, 589, 590, 601, and 608.

The Kestner factory was closed in 1938.

$$\mathcal{F}. \quad \begin{array}{c} made\ in \\ Germany. \end{array} \quad 10$$

$$211$$

$$J.D.K.$$

$$C \quad \begin{array}{c} made\ in \\ Germany \\ 152 \end{array} \quad 7$$

Kestner
Made in Germany

| D.R.G.M. 442910 |

| GERMANY |

5½

| **Excelsior** |
Germany 1

Max Kiesewetter & Co.
(see Erste Steinbacher
Porzellanfabrik)

Kimport Dolls
Independence, Missouri

Registered its trademark for dolls in 1937.

Kirchoff Werkstatt
Berlin-Halensee, Germany

Charlotte M. Kirchhoff made art dolls,
1925.

Kley & Hahn
Ohrdruf, Germany

Founded in 1902, Kley & Hahn manufactured leather and wood-bodied dolls and
celluloid dolls, as well as ball-jointed dolls
with bisque heads. Capitalizing on the
character doll boom, Kley & Hahn devoted
most of its efforts to the American market.
Some of its bisque heads were made by
other German companies, such as Kestner
(mold 200 & **Walküre**), Hertel, Schwab &
Co. (mold 100), and Bähr & Pröschild
(mold 500). **Majestic,** a walking doll, was
made by Kley & Hahn for Edmund Ulrich
Steiner.

Mold numbers found on Kley & Hahn
heads include: 100, 133, 135, 138, 158,
159, 160, 161, 162, 166, 167, 169, 180, 200,
250, 282, 292, 500, 520, 525, 526, 531,
546, 549, 554, 567, 571, and 680.

Among the trade names used were:

Cellunova (1913)

Dollar Princess (1909)
Durable (1909)
K (1909)
Majestic (1907)
Mein Einziges Baby (My Only Baby) (1913)
Meine Einzige (My Only One) (1910)
Princess (1909)
Schneewittchen (Snow White) (1910)
Special (Spezial for German market)
(c. 1909)
Walküre (1903)

C.F. Kling & Co.
Ohrdruf, Germany

Founded in 1834, this porcelain factory
began to produce dolls and dolls' heads
around 1870 and continued until the
1940s. Kling made china and bisque heads,
bathing dolls, and nanking dolls. It was one
of the few firms to make dolls' heads not
only with molded hair, but with additional
molded touches such as flowers, jewelry,
and clothing (around the neck) as well. The
additional molding serves as a good clue
in the identification of Kling dolls, especial-

ly early ones, whose heads were marked only with the mold number (the Kling **bell** trademark was introduced in 1880).

Kling used the following mold numbers: 116, 119, 122, 123, 124, 128, 129, 131, 133, 135, 140, 141, 142, 148, 151, 160, 167, 176, 185, 186, 188, 189, 190, 202, 203, 214, 216, 217, 220, 247, 254, 255, 285, 292, 293, 299, 303, 305, 370, 372, 373, and 377. [The 100 and 200 series were all shoulder heads, except for numbers 255, 292, 293, and 299, thought to have been made for Nöckler & Tittel.]

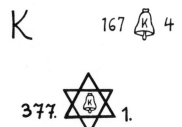

Kloster Veilsdorf
Veilsdorf on Werra, Germany

Nearly a century passed after the establishment of this porcelain factory in 1765 before it began to make dolls, but it became one of the largest German manufacturers of porcelain for the toy industry and made nanking dolls, bathing dolls, and dolls' heads until the late 1940s. Only a few dolls from this factory were marked; the entwined initials **CV** were used in several variations. Mold numbers include 500, 503, 532, and 900.

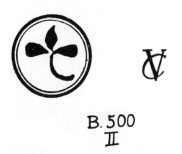

Erich Klötzer
Sonneberg, Germany

Founded in 1910, the Klötzer firm manufactured leather dolls and papier-mâché heads until c. 1930 (it used Buschow & Beck heads as well). Klötzer's mark appeared on the dolls' necks, simplifying identification, as a number of his creations from the late 1920s are uncannily similar to Käthe Kruse's earliest dolls.

Guido Knauth
Orlamünde, Germany

Founded in 1872; produced jointed dolls, doll parts, and character dolls (after 1910).

501-10

Knauth
3

Knell Brothers
(see Ludwig Greiner)

Edmund Knoch
Mönchröden, Germany

Founded in 1896; produced stuffed dolls with porcelain heads until the 1930s.

Gebrüder Knoch
Neustadt, Germany

Beginning in 1887, this doll factory produced bisque and china dolls' heads and composition doll parts. Gebrüder Knoch heads are sometimes unmarked. Marked heads are found with either the Gebrüder Knoch crossbones, Made in Germany/Ges. [mold number] Gesch., or simply with the mold number and Made in Germany. Numbers used were 179, 181, 190, 192, 193, 201, 203, 204, 205, 216, 217, 223, 230, and 232.

Gebrüder Knoch was purchased by Max Oscar Arnold in 1919 and ceased to manufacture dolls thereafter.

Made in Germany
206/7/0
D.R.G.M.

Made in Germany
Ges. N.° 216 Gesch.
15/0

Carl Knoll
Fischern, Bohemia

Founded in 1844; made dolls' heads c. 1901.

701
5

J. César Koch
Paris

Registered the trademarks Bébé Gloria and Lutecia Baby for dolls in 1915.

BÉBÉ GLORIA

Made in Paris

LUTECIA BABY

Made in Paris

König & Wernicke
Waltershausen, Germany

Founded in 1912 by Max König and Rudolf Wernicke, the firm manufactured jointed dolls, character dolls, bent-limb babies, hard rubber dolls (Hartgummi), and doll parts until at least 1935. Porcelain heads were supplied by Armand Marseille, Bähr & Pröschild, and Hertel, Schwab & Co.; celluloids, by Rheinische Gummi. König & Wernicke made My Playmate for Borgfeldt; its own trademarks included Der kleine Bösewicht (1916), Die Kleine Range (1916), and Mein Stolz (1914).

K & W
HARTGUMMI
555 0
GERMANY

Königliche Porzellanmanufaktur
Berlin

This porcelain factory, founded in 1761,

produced china shoulder heads, c. 1830-1870.

KPM   **K.P.M**

KPM

1844 - 1847.

1849—1870.

Königliche Porzellanmanufaktur

Meissen, Germany

The first porcelain factory to be established (1710), this firm produced dolls beginning around 1836. Known more familiarly as Meissen, the company incised its marks on the inside of the dolls' heads.

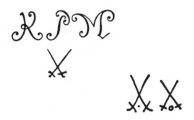

Kohl & Wengenroth

Offenbach, Germany

Founded in 1864, the company produced celluloid dolls, rubber dolls, bathing dolls, and character dolls during the first several decades of the 20th century.

M. Kohnstamm & Co.

Fürth, Sonneberg, and Olbernhau, Germany

Produced babies and jointed dolls from 1898 until at least 1930. Trademarks registered included **Cupid** (1908), **The Duchess Dressed Doll** (1915), **Lola** (1923), **Lydia** (1923), **Moko** (1898), **Mother Darling** (1910), **Nanette** (1926), and **Tessi** (1926). Some bisque heads were made for Kohnstamm by Hermann Steiner.

Else Lill Kolmar-Hecht

(see Else L. Hecht)

Konroe Merchants

New York City

In 1922, Konroe Merchants registered both its trademark and the trade name **My Honey**, which was used for a bisque-headed doll. It introduced **The Parisienne,** a flapper, in 1924.

Konstructo Co.

(see Mary Francis Woods)

Gustav Korn

Neu-Schmiedefeld, Germany

Founded in 1903, the firm produced bathing dolls during the first decade of the 20th century.

C. Krahmer
Frankenhausen, Germany

Advertised ball-jointed dolls and bent-limb babies, 1915.

G.K.
F.
66

Henri Othon Kratz-Boussac
Paris

Registered La Parisienne for dolls, 1910.

LA PARISIENNE

Werner Krauth
Leipzig, Germany

Manufactured dolls and dolls' heads, c. 1920.

Käthe Kruse
Bad Kösen, Germany

Kruse began making art dolls in 1904 and registered her name as a trademark in 1912. (The double K trademark was registered in 1923). Prior to World War II, all of her dolls were made by hand, of cheesecloth stuffed and delicately painted. After the War, the Käthe Kruse factory, still in operation today, was moved to Donäuworth and the dolls mass produced, resulting in a con-

siderable reduction in quality. Among the trade names Kruse introduced were **Du Mein** (1923), **Schlenkerchen** (1922), and **Träumerchen** (1923). The Kruse signature generally appears on the sole of one foot and a number on the other.

Schutz- Marke

Josef Kubelka
Vienna

Manufactured dolls and dolls' heads, 1884-1909.

4
B︠ SGDG

Gebrüder Kühnlenz
Kronach, Germany

Founded in 1884, this factory manufactured bisque and porcelain dolls (including swimming dolls) and dolls' heads. Until publication of the Ciesliks' *German Doll Encyclopedia,* Kühnlenz's marks had been falsely attributed to Gebrüder Krauss of Eisfeld, about whom little is actually known.

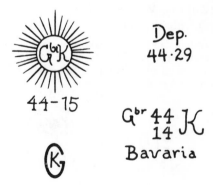

Dep.
44·29

44-15

G^{br} 44 K
14
Bavaria

L

Jacob Lacmann
Philadelphia

Made dolls' bodies, 1860-c. 1883; used heads by Ludwig Greiner and Cuno & Otto Dressel.

André Laffitte
Paris

Made dolls' heads and eyes, 1917.

" VITA "

Cecile Lambert
La Garenne-Colombes, France

Using the business name of Edmée Rozier, Cecile Lambert registered **Babet** as a trademark for dolls in 1921.

BABET

Leopold Lambert
Paris

Made and exported mechanical dolls, as well as dolls in glass cases, 1888-1923; used **L.B.** as a mark.

L.B.

Lambert & Samhammer
Sonneberg, Germany

Produced dolls and dolls' heads between 1872 and 1881. The trademark shown was registered in 1876.

Hermann Landshut & Co.
Waltershausen, Germany

Founded in 1892; registered **Linon** as trademark, 1895, when name was changed to I. Eisenstaedt & Co. Trademark in use until at least 1902.

Alfred Lange
Friedrichroda, Germany

Registered his trademark, **May Blossom,** in 1923.

A. Lanternier & Cie.
Limoges, France

The bisque heads of Lanternier, made between 1891 and c. 1925, have been found
incised **Lorraine, La Georgienne,** and
Favorite. Several marks used by Lanternier
are shown here; the identities of **Ed. Tasson**
and **T. E. Maskon** are uncertain.

FABRICATION
FRANÇAISE

FAVORITE

N° ²/₀

Ed Tasson

ALECⁱᵉ
LIMOGES

FABRICATION
FRANÇAISE

ALECⁱᵉ
LIMOGES
A   1

LIMOGES
A L

J.E.Maskon
SG
LORRAINE
No
A.L.&Cⁱᵉ
LIMOGES

Laquionie & Cie.
Paris

Registered three trademarks for dolls, 1919.

JOLI GUY

ROSETTE

MUGUETTE

Howard R. Larsen
Milwaukee, Wisconsin

Registered the trade name **Jiggle Wiggle**
c. 1921-1922; the name was stamped on the
doll.

Lawrence & Co.
(see Cocheco Manufacturing Co.)

Le Montréer
Paris

Distributors of dolls from 1867 to c. 1921;
registered **Le Trottin** (1913) and **Le Vic-
torieux** (1914) as trademarks for dolls and
bébés.

LE TROTTIN

LE VICTORIEUX

Ange Le Prince
Paris

Registered **Scaramouche** as a trademark for
dolls, 1924.

Madame Lebel
Paris

Registered **Patria** as a trademark for dressed
dolls, 1915.

PATRIA

H. LeConte & Co.
Paris

Information about this firm is scant. H.
LeConte & Co. is known to have exhibited
dolls at the 1900 Paris Exposition and may
possibly be the same firm that began as
Leconte & Alliot in 1866. A known doll
by H. LeConte & Co. has a papier-mâché

body and a bisque head. The head is incised as shown below.

Alexandre Lefebvre & Cie.
Lagny, France

From 1863 to c. 1921; made *bébés incassables* and papier-mâché babies, including the trade name **Bébé A.L.** (1912).

Leibe & Hofmann
Gera-Untermhaus, Germany

Porcelain factory established in 1772; produced dolls and dolls' heads, 1882-1888.

Louis-Aimé Lejeune
Saint-Maur-des-Fosses, France

Registered his trademark in 1915 for dolls and doll parts.

Yvonne Lelièvre
Paris

Registered the trademark **Lisette** for dolls in 1922.

Lenci
Turin, Italy

Using the trade name **Lenci**, Enrico Scavini produced pressed-felt dolls beginning c. 1920. His dolls came in a wide range of styles and represented a variety of characters. **Fad-Ette** (1923) was the trade name of one of his dolls. Some Lenci dolls can be identified by a paper label or metal button affixed to them; others had a mark stamped on the foot. Unmarked Lencis were more common and can be easily confused with similar dolls made by other firms.

Lenox Inc.
Trenton, New Jersey

Primarily a pottery company, the firm established by Walter Scott Lenox made some bisque dolls' heads for Effanbee, c. 1914-1920.

Lenox
Effanbee
16

Lerch & Co.
Philadelphia

From 1866 to 1870, Philip Lerch, a toy maker, manufactured dolls' heads. His company name, as shown, appeared on a label affixed to the head. Another label has been found which bears the company name of **Lerch and Klag;** the identity of Klag is not known.

Lerch & Co.
MANUFACTURERS
No.7.

Les Arts du Papier
Paris

Registered two trademarks in 1919 for composition dolls and dolls' heads.

LA MIGNONNE

Les Bébés de France Cie.
Paris

Made plastic dolls, 1919. The French slogan means "and if I fall, I won't break."

"... et si je tombe, je ne casse pas"

Elizabeth Lesser
New York City

Among the dolls Lesser copyrighted were Isabel (1912), Leonie (1912), Mary Elizabeth (1911), **1914 Girl** (1914), **Red Cross Nurse** (1917), **Sister to Mary Elizabeth** (1912), **War Baby** (1915), and **A Young American** (1913).

H. J. Leven
Sonneberg, Germany

Brought about by the merger of Hugo Dressel and Leven & Sprenger in 1912, the Leven firm produced leather dolls, babies, dolls' heads and doll parts until at least 1938. The firm used heads by Armand Marseille.

Edmond Levi
Neuilly-sur-Seine, and Paris

Manufactured jointed plastic dolls and registered the trademark **Les Poupées de France** in 1919.

LES POUPÉES DE FRANCE

Albert Levy
Paris

Registered the trade name **Tanagra,** 1917.

TANAGRA

Pierre Lévy & Cie.
Paris

Registered **Bébé Bijou** as a trade name in 1919.

Louis L'Heureux
Paris

Registered his surname as a trademark for dolls, 1905.

Ernst Liebermann
Neustadt, Germany

Founded in 1894, this factory produced jointed dolls and talking dolls with celluloid heads. Trade names used included **Adelene** (1927), **Baby Joan** (1927), **EL** (1930), **Eli** (1930), and **Violet** (1927).

Liegnitzer Puppenfabrik
Liegnitz, Germany

This doll factory was founded in 1869 by

Moritz Pappe. It produced dolls of wood, leather, wool, and other materials until the late 1920s.

Michel Lilienthal
Paris

Registered **Miss Dancing** as a trademark for dolls, 1922.

MISS DANCING

Limbach, AG.
Limbach, Germany

Established in 1772 by Gotthelf Greiner, the porcelain factory produced mainly household pottery and animal figures until the 1880s, when it began to make dolls' heads, jointed dolls, and bathing dolls. The manufacture of dolls' heads, a specialty, was discontinued in 1899 and only resumed in 1919, when the trade names **Norma, Rita,** and **Wally** began to appear as part of the Limbach mark, along with the **cloverleaf** and **crown.** Mold numbers attributed to Limbach include 2780, 6335, 8552, 8553, 8660, 8675, 8682, 8822, 8867, 9027, and 9307. The number 10,000, registered in 1913, denoted the entire line of Limbach dolls and toys rather than one particular mold. The firm was still in operation as late as 1937.

GERMANY
8822

Louis Lindner & Söhne
Sonneberg, Germany

A reincarnation of the firm of Louis & Edward Lindner (founded in 1833), this Sonneberg company was reopened in 1847 and offered wooden, leather, and stuffed dolls and doll parts with papier-mâché, wax, or porcelain heads. The trade name **Baby Bunting** was registered in 1887; as indicated by the mark shown, Simon & Halbig made heads for Lindner, which was in business until 1929. Mold number attributed to this company is 1339.

1339
S&H
LL&S
10½

Lippert & Haas
Schlaggenwald, Bohemia

Founded in 1792, this porcelain factory made dolls' heads as early as 1845. It was renamed Haas & Czjzek in 1867. The two-digit number included in the firm's incised mark refers to the date the doll was made (for example, the 60 on the mark shown indicates that the doll was made in 1860).

/S
60

Live Long Toys
Chicago

Starting in 1923, Live Long Toys manufactured rag dolls and all-bisque dolls based on cartoonist Frank O. King's characters from the "Gasoline Alley" comic strip. The names included **Mrs. Blossom, Puff, Rachel, Skeezix,** and **Uncle Walt.** An oilcloth Mrs. Blossom doll bears a printed mark, as follows: —**King**—//**MRS. BLOSSOM**//**PAT. APPLIED FOR.** Live Long Toys also made a **Little Orphan Annie** doll (1925) based on Harold Gray's cartoon character.

Loeffler & Dill
Sonneberg, Germany

Produced dolls' heads and jointed dolls, c. 1886-1932.

L & D
6/0
X

Anni Lonz
Coblenz, Germany

Registered the trademark **Alah** for dolls, 1924.

Geneviève Loudouze
Paris

Registered the trademark **Ninon** for dolls, 1925.

"NINON"

Madame Louit
Bordeaux, France

Registered **Poupées Gauloises** as a trademark for dolls, 1916.

POUPÉES
GAULOISES

Joseph Love, Inc.
New York City

Registered a trademark for dolls in 1935.

Princess
Elizabeth

Julienne Lubecka
Paris

Registered **Bicot** as a trademark for dolls, 1926.

BICOT

A. Luge & Co.
Sonneberg, Germany

Founded in 1881, Luge produced kid dolls and character dolls until at least 1930. It used the trade names **Pat-a-Cake** (1912) and **South Sea Baby** (1928). Dolls' heads were supplied by Ernst Heubach, Gebrüder Heubach, and Armand Marseille. The mark shown here was Luge's trademark; the mark incised on the head will be only that of the head's maker. Known mold numbers supplied by these makers include 351, 353, 362 (Marseille); H 33, 380, 396, 399, 444 (Ernst Heubach); and 6736 (Gebrüder Heubach).

Thuringia

Trade   mark.

Eg. M. Luthardt
Steinach, Germany

Founded in 1868, the firm made leather,

imitation leather, and felt dolls until at least the 1930s; used the mark **Luta** during its last decade.

Germany

Louis Philipp Luthard
Neustadt, Germany

Established in 1909; advertised stuffed dolls and jointed dolls in 1921.

Lyro-Puppen-Company
Berlin

Some confusion exists regarding the **Lyro** trademark within the six-pointed star shown here. It is attributed both to Lyro-Puppen-Company and to Rolfes & Co., both of Berlin, and in both cases was registered in 1923 for cloth dolls. Franz Volpert, also of Berlin, registered the same trademark in 1925.

M

E. Maar & Sohn
Mönchröden, Germany

Produced bisque-headed character babies, 1910-c. 1930. Used Armand Marseille heads.

Made in Germany
Armand Marseille
256
A 4/0 M
Maar

Ma.E. Maar, KG
Mönchröden, Germany

Founded in 1920, the firm produced bisque dolls until c. 1930.

Robert Maaser
Sonneberg, Germany

Made bisque, composition, and celluloid dolls' heads, c. 1904-c. 1930.

Germany
410
5/0

Louise Adrienne Mabit
Paris

Registered the trademarks Janus and Les Deux Gosses for dolls' heads and dolls, 1925.

JANUS

LES DEUX GOSSES

Madame Georgene Inc.
(see Averill Manufacturing Co.)

Maiden Toy Co. (Maiden America Toy Manufacturing Co.)
New York City

Made dolls, 1915-1919. Produced Maiden America dolls for which the trademark was registered by designer Katherine Silverman (1915); used the initial MAT for character dolls in 1919.

Maiden

America

Manufacture des Bébés et Poupées
Paris

Made bébés incassables, using the trademark La Madelon, 1919.

LA MADELON

Charles Marcoux
Montreuil-sous-Bois, France

Registered his trademark in 1920 for dolls and dolls' heads.

Pauline Margulies
Brooklyn, New York

Registered **Empress** as a trademark for dolls, 1933.

EMPRESS

Maurice Mariage
Paris

Registered **La Poupée Lina** as a trademark for dolls, 1923.

LA POUPÉE LINA

Marienfeld
Ölze, Germany

Founded in 1892, this porcelain factory made doll parts and nanking dolls with porcelain or bisque heads. Marienfeld went into bankruptcy in 1903 and its assets were purchased by Hertwig & Co.

<M>

Marks Brothers Co.
Boston

Made and imported celluloid socket- and shoulder-heads, from 1918 into the 1920s.

Armand Marseille
Köppelsdorf and Neuhaus, Germany

Armand Marseille bought a toy factory in 1884 and a porcelain factory in 1885 and started to produce porcelain jugs and pipe heads. He began making shoulderheads c. 1890 and in 1893 registered the first of a series of anchor trademarks, placed within a circle, with the initials **AM** flanking it. The anchor incorporating the initial **W** was used exclusively for dolls' heads made for Louis Wolf; the stylized anchor with the initials **AM** connected to it was introduced in 1910, and the last anchor mark shown c. 1920.

Marseille's bisque heads were made both for his own company and for other firms, such as Bergmann, Borgfeldt, Cuno & Otto Dressell, and Otto Gans. (The **AM** initials are often used in conjunction with the other firms' mark.) Armand Marseille heads vary widely in quality and many of the molds designed were used for several decades and in varying materials, making precise dating difficult without expert advice. It is known, however, that dolls' heads marked **DRGM** were made starting in 1909; those marked **DRMR** appeared after 1910. Through the years, Armand Marseille used scores of different marks, but even the novice collector can recognize the initials **AM** that appear on almost every Marseille mark.

Early numbers found on Marseille heads were, in fact, years: 1890, 1892, 1893, 1894, 1895, 1896, 1897, 1898, 1899, 1900, 1901, 1902, 1903, 1905, and 1909. Other four-digit numbers found on the company's bisque heads are thought to have been introduced between 1895 and 1899: 2000, 2010, 2015, 3000, 3091, 3093, 3200, 3500, 3600, 3700, and 4008.

Mold numbers identified as coming from the Marseille factory have been further identified as to year of first manufacture (though, to repeat, many of them were in use for a number of years after first being issued). In 1910, Marseille introduced 500, 504, 505, 510, 513, 515, 516, 518, 519, 520, 540, 542, 550, 550A, 551, 551k, 560, 560A, 570, 590, 599, 600, 620, 621, 630,

640a, 670, 696, 700, 701, 710, 711, 800, 810, 820, 900, 920, 927, 950, 951, 966, and 970.

In 1911 the following numbers were added: 200, 205, 210, 223, and 230.

In 1912 these first appeared: 231, 233, 240, 242, 244, 246, 250, 251, 252, 390a, 391, 395, 396, 398, and 399.

In 1913: 320, 322, 323, 324, 325, 326, 327, 328, 329, 333, 341, 341k, 341ka, 342, 345, 350, 351, 351k, 352, 353, 356, 360a, 362, 369, 370, 371, 372, 375, 376, 377, 378, 382, 384, 390, 750, 760, 790, 971, 971a, 972, 973, 975, 980, 984, 985, 990, 991, 992, 993, 995, 996, 997, 1231, 1330, 3333, 1335, 1369, 1370, and 1374.

In 1925: 253, 254, 255, 256, 259, 266, 270, 273, 275, 276, 300, 309, 310, and 318.

And in 1926: 400, 401, 406, 411, 414, 449, 450, 451, 452, 452H, 454, and 458.

In addition to the fact that many molds were recycled and reused over a period of years, there does not seem to be any numerical or chronological pattern to Marseille's choice of the numbers it assigned in a given year. The 400 series, for example, was not introduced until 1926, while the 500 series was first used in 1910.

Among the trade names Marseille used on its character babies and dolly-faced dolls' heads (exclusively for export to the United States were:

Alma (1900)
Baby Betty (1912—see mark)
Baby Gloria (1910)
Baby Phyllis (1925)
Beauty (1898)
Cama
Columbia (1904)
Darling
Duchess (1914)
Ellar Baby (c.1925—see mark)
Fany (1912)
Florodora (1903—see marks)
Just Me (c.1910)
Kiddiejoy (1920)
Lilly (c.1913)
Lissy
Little Sister (1911)
Mabel (see mark)
Majestic (1902—designed by Edmund Steiner)

Margaret
My Dream Baby (1925)
My Playmate (c.1907)
Nobbikid (1914)
Our Pet (c.1926)
Princess (c.1900)
Queen Louise (1910)
Rosebud (1902)

Note: The names of these bisque dolls are almost always incised on the heads.

A.M.
Germany.
341/1K.

Made in Germany

A [Baby o Betty] M

D.R.G.M.

Made in Germany
Armand Marseille
560a
A %0 M
D.R.M.R.232

A [ELLAR star] M

Germany
8 ½

Made in Germany

Florodora

A 4 M

Germany.
Mabel

François-Emile Marseille
Maisons Alfort, France

Made **Le Petit Français**, a jointed bébé incassable, 1888.

Charles Marsh
London

Produced poured-wax and papier-mâché dolls from 1878 until 1894; his distributor was C. Gooch, whose name sometimes appears on Marsh's mark.

Edith Maus
Brunswick, Germany

Registered the trademarks **Edith Maus** and **Rompers** in 1925 for cloth dolls and jointed rubber dolls.

Maxine Doll Co.
New York City.

Registered **Baby Gloria** as a trademark for dolls in 1929

May Frères, Cie.
Paris

Registered **Bébé Mascotte** for fully jointed dolls, 1890. (Jules Steiner may have purchased May Frères after 1897, since he advertised Bébé Mascotte.)

BÉBÉ MASCOTTE

The Mechanical Rubber Co.
New York City, Chicago, and Cleveland

Founded in 1915; produced a variety of rubber character dolls, including **Sailor, Clown,** and **Uncle Sam.** Became part of the United States Rubber Co. after 1917, when the **shield** mark was registered.

Herbert John Meech
London

Meech was the Royal Family's doll-maker from 1865 until 1891, and made wax dolls and composition dolls. Mark found on bodies of wax dolls.

Meissen
(see Konigliche Porzellanmanufaktur)

Minnie M. Meldram
New York City

Registered her trademark, **Soxie,** in 1920

Metal Doll Co.
Pleasantville, New Jersey

Produced **All Steel Dolls,** 1902. Mark found on bodies.

```
PATENTS PENDING
    MADE BY
METAL DOLL CO.,
Pleasantville, N.J.
```

Ernst Metzler
Pressig-Rothenkirchen, Germany

Porcelain factory founded in 1909, produced porcelain and composition heads from at least 1924 until the early 1940s.

Made in Germany
Metzler
890
E ³/₀M

Gebrüder Metzler & Ortloff
Ilmenau, Germany

Produced porcelain dolls' heads, c. 1893-1903.

Amandus Michaelis
Rauenstein and Sonneberg, Germany; and Brussels

A doll factory founded in 1870; produced leather dolls and bodies, jointed dolls, and dolls of papier-mâché from c. 1890 to 1918 and again from 1922 into the 1930s. Registered the trade name **Michel** in 1911. While the **AM** in the mark is sometimes confused with Armand Marseille, the Marseille firm never enclosed the initials within a triangle.

Millikin & Lawley
London

Distributed cloth dolls and knitted dolls, some with porcelain heads and limbs, 1881-1882, including **Charity Girl, Lilliputian Dolls, Little Red Riding Hood, Miss Rosebud,** and **Scotch Boy.**

Mimosa
Ochenbruck and Neuhaus, Germany

In 1923, registered a trademark for its range of character dolls, bent-limb babies, and dressed dolls.

J.R. Miranda & Co.
Oregon City, Oregon

Produced Indian dolls in 1919, including **Buck, Chief, Little Buck, Little Princess, Madonna, Papoose,** and **Squaw.**

Modern Toy Co.
Brooklyn, New York

Manufactured unbreakable character dolls from 1914 to the 1920s. **Buttercup** (1924), a rag doll, was based on Jimmy Murphy's character in the "Toots and Casper" cartoon strip. Among Modern Toys' other trade names were **Babbit at Your Service** (1916), **Cleanser Boy** (1916), **Co-Ed** (1915), **College Boy** (1915), and **Petite Polly** (1915).

August Möller & Sohn
Georgenthal, Germany

Founded in 1915; manufactured dolls' heads and other doll parts. Registered the trademark **Amuso** in 1925. Among the known mold numbers used by the firm were 100 and 1920.

Möller & Dippe
Unterköditz, Germany

Founded in 1879, this porcelain factory produced dolls' heads and arms by at least 1893; by 1913 the majority of dolls produced were pincushion dolls. Note the similarity of Möller & Dippe's **anchor** trademark (registered in 1892) and those of Armand Marseille.

$$M.|D.$$
$$U.$$

Marie Mommessin
(see Madame E. Cayette)

Montanari
London

The Montanari family made wax dolls from 1851 until the 1870s. Montanari dolls are typically chubby, with folds of fat under the chin and on the arms. They were created more for wealthy children than for the general public. Many of the company's dolls are not marked; in addition to the marks presented here, the Montanaris were known to have used **Mty**; the name has been found spelled **Montanary** as well. The marks appear on the doll's body.

Montanari
Manufacturer.
251 Regent St.
and 180 Soho Bazaar

Montanari
180 Soho Bazaar
London

Montgomery Ward & Co.
Chicago

This department store distributed dolls made by Kestner, Horsman, Schoenhut, and other firms. In 1901, it advertised cloth dolls with **Silesia Doll Bodies**; in 1925, imitation kid bodies called **Kidiline**. Its **diamond-shaped** trademark was registered in 1915. Among the names of dolls it sold between 1887 and 1930 were:

Adeline (1916)
American Lady (1901)
American Maid (1900)
Baby Bright (1912)
Baby Ella (1916)
Baby Hilda (1916)
Dolly Dimples (1916)
Goodie-Goodie (1916)
Kutie-Kiddies (1916)
Little Ethel (1916)
The Little Patriot (1916)
Little Red Riding Hood (1916)
Merry Miss (1916)
Miss Mabel (1916)
Molly-O (1916)
Mother Hubbard (1901)
Pauline (1916)
Pretty Baby (1916)

Princess Helen (1916)
Sweet Susan (1916)

Moore & Gibson Corp.
United States

In 1917, made leather, imitation leather, and fabric dolls, including **Balsam Dolls**, **Carriage Dolls**, **Floating Dolls**, and **Mailing Dolls**.

Moran Doll Manufacturing Co.
Los Angeles and San Francisco; Kansas City, Missouri

Between 1919 and 1921, made various baby dolls, some designed by Julius Benvenuti. Among its trade names were **Blinkie Doll** (1920), **Blynke** (1919), **Bobette** (1920), **Cry Blynkie** (1920), and **Wee Wee** (1920).

Morimura Brothers
New York City

The Japanese import house of Morimura Brothers supplied Japanese-made bisque-headed dolls to American customers during and immediately after World War I (the flow of bisque dolls from Europe had virtually ceased at the outbreak of the war). Morimura also sold nanking and **Kidolyn**-bodied-dolls and distributed dolls made by American firms, including Bester Doll Manufacturing Company (**The Bester Doll**). One variant of Morimura's **MB** mark is shown (it was incised on the head). Some trade names used by the company, sometimes appearing on a label affixed to the dolls' stomach, included:

Baby Darling or My Darling (1919—see mark)
Baby Ella (1919)
Baby O'Mine (1920)

Baby Rose (1919)
The Bester Doll (1918)
Dolly Doll (1919)
First Prize Baby (1919)
My Sweetheart (1920)
Queue San Baby (1916—see mark)

Carl Moritz
Taubenbach, Germany

This porcelain factory was founded in 1840, but was not known to have made dolls until 1888. After 1893, the factory's production was concentrated on toys and knickknacks.

same address in 1870 and used it on his stickers.]

CHARLES MORRELL
50 BURLINGTON ARCADE
LONDON

Alexandre Mothereau
Paris

The **B.M.** trademark shown was incised on a ball-jointed doll called **Bébé Mothereau,** made by this company from 1880 to 1896.

6.
B.M.

Mothers' Congress Doll Co.
Philadelphia

Made rag dolls from 1900 to 1911; **Baby Stuart** was introduced in 1900. The mark appeared on the back of the torso.

Charles Morrell
London

A retailer, exporter, and importer, the Morrell firm was established in 1878 and sold Pierotti wax dolls as well as German and French creations until the 1920s. The company's mark was generally stamped on the doll's torso. [The doll-maker Horace W. Morrell, perhaps a predecessor, was at the

Christoph Motschmann
Sonneberg, Germany

According to Jürgen and Marianne Cieslik's meticulous research, it is likely that Christoph Motschmann received the first patent for a talking doll mechanism, one that could be mass-produced fairly inexpensively for insertion into the doll's body. The stamp shown has been found on talking dolls produced between 1857 and 1859, the operative patent years, though there is no proof that Motschmann made the dolls in which the mechanism was used.

Andreas Müller
Sonneberg and Coburg, Germany

Founded in 1887; produced nanking, wax, and wooden dolls and doll bodies, 1894-1928. (The crown trademark was registered in 1896, the windmill with figures in 1922, after the firm moved to Coburg.)

Karl Müller & Co.
Effelder, Germany

Made stuffed dolls and babies with bisque heads, c. 1923-1928.

Pierre Muller
Levallois, France

Registered the trademark Olympia in 1924.

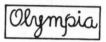

W. G. Müller
Sonneberg, Germany

Founded in 1900, this factory assembled dolls using bodies from a Neustadt firm and bisque heads from Armand Marseille (mold number 390) or celluloid ones from Rheinische Gummi, marked with that firm's famous turtle mark. Its major American customer was Louis Wolf. Müller's **Weegem** trademark, incorporating the firm's initials, **W.G.M.**, was registered in 1930.

Müller & Kaltwasser
Rauenstein, Germany

Made cloth dolls, c.1927-c.1935.

Müller & Strasburger
Sonneberg, Germany

Produced dolls of papier mâché and porcelain, c. 1884-1892. The sticker shown was used on papier-mâché shoulder heads; other numbers used were 1020, 2020, and 4515.

Maison Munnier
Paris

Manufactured wax and papier-mâché dolls, 1834-1852. The mark shown was found on a doll's body.

N

A. Nadaud
Paris

Sold dolls, 1878-c. 1890, including some with bisque heads by Simon & Halbig (S & H's popular mold 1079 was prevalent). The Nadaud mark was used both as a sticker and as a stamp on the dolls' bodies.

Hippolyte Naneau
Paris

Registered the trademark Gentil Bébé in 1905.

CENTIL BÉBÉ

National Joint-Limb Doll Co.
New York City

Produced papier-mâché dolls, 1917-1922. Registered NAJO as a trademark in 1917

and advertised Miss Najo dolls. Mark is found on doll's torso.

Mabel Drake Nekarda
New York City

Nekarda's trademarks, Suffragette Kid and Votes-for-Women, were registered in 1911. She stipulated that the trademarks were to be used on labels affixed to the dolls.

Nelke Corp.
Philadelphia

Made knitted dolls, 1917-1925; the trademark (1925) appeared on a ribbon label. Among the dolls Nelke advertised were The Cop (1923), Diggeldy Dan (1923), The Imp (1923), Nelke Boy (1921), Nelke Clown (1921), and Nelke Dollies (1918).

Neumann & Marx
(see Société Industrielle de Celluloid)

New Era Novelty Co. (Nenco)
Newark, New Jersey

Produced jointed composition dolls, 1914-1916. In 1915, introduced the trade names **Our Baby, S'Kooter Kid,** and **YamaYama Doll.**

New Era Toy & Novelty Co.
Newark, New Jersey

In 1921, manufactured **Kimball** boy and girl dolls, as well as **Flirt** and **Cherie** dolls, all of which were cherub-like. [No connection has been found between New Era Toy & Novelty and New Era Novelty Company, both of Newark.]

New Toy Manufacturing Co.
New York City and Newark, New Jersey

Founded before 1912, New Toy Manufacturing Company claimed to be America's largest doll factory by 1917. It specialized in composition character dolls (using the trademark **Nutoi** by 1918, though it wasn't registered until 1920) and in a new material, registered in 1915, which it called **Lignumfibro.** Among the many trade names advertised by the company were:

Bride (1919)
Bridesmaid (1919)
Coquette (1912)
Kupid (1919)
Maytime Girl (1919)
Merry Widow (1919)

Midolly (1919)
Newbisc, the World's Doll (1919—see marks)
Peggy (1919)
Phyllis May (1920)

New York Rubber Co.
New York City

Made rubber dolls under Goodyear's patent, 1851-1917.

NEWYORK RUBBER CO.
GOODYEAR'S PAT. 444

Nöckler & Tittel
Schneeberg, Germany

Founded in 1849, the Nöckler & Tittel factory manufactured a wide range of dolls and dolls' heads after 1886. Materials included composition, rubber, wood, and wool. Bisque heads were ordered from Armand Marseille (mold numbers included 370, 375, 390, and 391), Alt, Beck & Gottschalk, and Hertel, Schwab & Co. (molds in the 100 series). The firm's initials were incised on character heads; its **Schneeflöckchen** (little snowflake) trademark was registered in 1923.

Charles Marie Paul Noël
Saint-Etienne, France

Registered **Marquisette** as a trademark, 1923.

Non-Breakable Doll Co.
Pawtucket, Rhode Island

Made dolls, 1912-1916. Registered **Jam Kiddo** (1915) as a trademark and advertised more than thirty different dolls, including **Clownee, Red Riding Hood, Sailor Boy, Sweet Lavender,** and **Toddles.**

Non-Breakable Toy Co.
Milwaukee and Muskegon, Michigan

Produced **Capo** line of unbreakable composition dolls, 1916-1917.

Nonbreakable Toy Co.
New York City

Advertised **Mar-sell-ene,** a clown doll, and the **Kandy Twins,** 1911-1912.

Leo Nordschild
Berlin

Founded in 1878, the Nordschild firm manufactured art dolls, jointed and walking dolls, and character babies during the 1920s, some with Kämmer & Reinhardt heads. It registered **Bella Puppen** as a trademark in 1924.

Nikolaus Oberender
Öslau, Germany

The company produced bisque dolls' heads from its establishment in 1910 until at least the late 1920s. Its entwined **NO** mark was incised on the heads, along with a mold number. Among the numbers used were 125, 2000, and 2010.

$$\mathcal{N}$$
$$\textit{Germany}$$
$$125$$
$$8/0$$

H. Offenbacher & Co.
Nuremberg, Germany

Founded in 1919; registered **Oco** as a trademark in 1921 for cloth dolls, jointed dolls, bent-limb babies, and toddlers. The mark appeared on a ribbon attached to the foot.

Gebrüder Ohlhaver
Sonneberg, Germany

Gebrüder Ohlhaver introduced its famous **Revalo** trademark in 1913 (the word derived from the Ohlhaver name spelled backwards phonetically); conflicting sources give the factory's founding date as 1897 and 1912. As the marks shown indicate, Ohlhaver ordered heads from other German makers, including Ernst Heubach, Gebrüder Heubach, and Porzellanfabrik Mengersgereuth (the X within the **circle**). The word **Igodi** used on one of the marks shown refers to a patented swivel head invented by Johann Gottlieb Dietrich in 1919; such heads were also produced by Ernst Heubach. In 1921, Ohlhaver introduced **My Queen Doll** and **Bébé Princesse.** Known mold numbers include 10727 and 11010.

Heubach · Köppefsclorf.
Jgodi.
Revalo · 22 · 11
Germany.

Fernand Paulin Olivier
Mézières, France

Registered the trademark **A la Clinique des Poupées,** 1920.

Rose O'Neill
Wilkes-Barre, Pennsylvania

Rose O'Neill's whimsical line drawings of fairy-like **Kewpies** first appeared in the *Ladies Home Journal* in 1909; their instant popularity resulted in a tidal wave of dolls, designed by O'Neill with the supervision of Joseph Kallus (see Cameo Doll Co.), which began to appear in 1912. By the beginning of World War I, some twenty-one factories in Germany and the United States were manufacturing Kewpies to meet the demand of the George Borgfeldt Co., which distributed them exclusively after 1916. Borgfeldt ordered all-bisque Kewpies from Kestner, Gebrüder Voight, Hermann Voight, and other porcelain factories. Celluloids came from Karl Standfuss; cloth Kewpies from Steiff; and composition ones from Cameo Doll Co., among others. Most Kewpies had O'Neill's signature molded on one foot; heart-shaped or circular stickers appeared on the chests. It is difficult to tell which company made which Kewpie, however, since with the exception of Kallus's Cameo Doll Co., few of the firms manufacturing the doll used their own marks. And because of the doll's popularity, there were many unauthorized imitations made.

O'Neill designed a follow-up to the Kewpie, **Scootles,** in 1925; its name, or Rose O'Neill, was incised on the sole of the foot.

SCOOTLES

Jeanne I. Orsini
New York City

During the late teens and the early 1920s, Orsini designed a number of small character dolls, most of which had cheery, smiling expressions. Some all-bisque versions of her designs were manufactured by Alt, Beck & Gottschalk (theirs is the JIO © 1920 mark); some of them were also distributed by Borgfeldt. Among the trade names Orsini introduced were:

Didi (1920)
Dodo (1916)
Fifi (1918)

Mimi (1920)
Nellie Sunshine (1918)
Tummyache (1916)
Uncle Sam (1919)
Vivi (1920—see mark, used as sticker)
Zizi (1920)
Known mold numbers include 1429, 1430, and 1440.

Copr. By
J.J. Orsini
Germany

J. I. O. © 1920
44

Oz Doll & Toy Manufacturing Co.
Los Angeles

Frank Baum, author of **The Wizard of Oz** (1900), registered a trademark for dolls in 1924.

P

Madame Pannier
Paris

Between 1872 and 1892, Madame Pannier made dolls and doll accessories and was one of Jumeau's representatives. The CP mark (for Charles Pannier, thought to be

a relative) was incised on heads; the other found on the sole of the foot.

C9P.

Mme. Pannier

Pápa Pottery
Hungary

This earthenware firm, founded in 1811, was known to have made dolls as well as pottery.

PAPA

Gebrüder Paris
Oberköditz, Germany

Founded in 1886; produced bathing dolls between c. 1898 and 1938. Trademark registered in 1910, though used since 1907.

Parsons-Jackson Co.
Cleveland

Parsons-Jackson developed and introduced **Biskoline**, a celluloid-like material, in 1910 and registered it in 1913. In the same year, it registered two other trademarks—the initials **KKK** and the figure of a **stork**, which has been found both on dolls' heads and on bodies (with the addition of the company name and location). The firm's slogan was **Kant Krak.**

THE PARSONS-JACKSON CO.
CLEVELAND, OHIO.

Peacock's
London

Distributed composition and wax dolls, c. 1862.

From
PEACOCK'S
The Beaming Nurse
525 NEW OXFORD ST.
Corner of Bloomsbury St.
LONDON, W.C.

Pean Frères
(see Chambre Syndicale des Fabricants de Jouets Français)

Mrs. Lucy Peck
London

Made and sold dolls at her shop, called The Doll's Home or The Doll's House, 1891-1921. Variants of her mark are found stamped on wax dolls' bodies.

E. Pelletier
Marseilles, France

Manufactured and exported bébés, some with wooden heads, from 1890 to 1900. The trademark shown, registered in 1892, was used on boxes containing the dolls.

Hermann Pensky
Eisfeld and Coburg, Germany

Produced mama dolls, stuffed dolls, and walking dolls, c. 1925. The **Pehaco** mark is a phonetic representation in German of the letters "P" and "H" plus the abbreviation of "company."

Pehaco
Hannelore
85

Perfect Toy Manufacturing Co.
New York City

Made composition dolls, 1919-1920s. **Baby Betty**, a trade name, was used beginning in 1919. **Perfect** was inscribed on the shoulder plate.

PERFECT

Henry Perier
Paris

Registered **M.P.** and **La Vraie Parisienne** as trademarks for dolls, 1916.

La Vraie Parisienne

Gaston Perrimond
Nice, France

Registered the trademark **La Poupée Nicette** for cloth dolls, 1924.

Madame Perrin
Paris

Registered **La Poupée des Alliés** and **L.P.A.** as trademarks for dolls, 1916.

La Poupée des Alliés

M. Pessner & Co.
New York City

Registered **Sistie Doll** as a trademark for dolls, 1934.

Petit & Dumontier
Paris

Manufacturers of dolls and bébés, 1878-1890. The mark **P + D**, incised on bisque heads, has been attributed to the firm, but not yet proved.

Petit & Mardochée
Fountainbleau, France

Made porcelain heads, c. 1843-1860. The mark shown includes the initials of the founder, Jacob Petit; it was incised on dolls' heads.

Petitcollin
Paris, Etain, and Lilas, France

Established in 1914, the firm made celluloid dolls.

Dr. Dora Petzold
Berlin

Began making cloth art dolls with composition heads in 1919; registered Dora Petzold as a trademark in 1920, D.P. and girl within circle in 1924.

Schutz-Marke

Fritz Pfeffer
Gotha, Germany

Fritz Pfeffer took over an existing porcelain factory in 1892. He made dolls' heads, bathing dolls, nanking dolls, and doll parts until at least 1930. The PG mark probably stands for "Pfeffer/Gotha."

Margaret B. Philips
Port Allegany, Pennsylvania

Registered a trademark, **Polly Preparedness Patriotic Person**, 1916.

Pierotti
London

The Pierotti family made finely modeled wax dolls' heads beginning about 1789 and by 1850 was offering composition and papier-mâché dolls as well. (Most examples of the firm's work likely to be found today were made after 1880). Pierotti heads were combined with stuffed bodies also made by the family; the mark shown, incised on the back of the neck, is rare, since most London dealers who handled the dolls used their own marks instead.

Emil Pfeiffer
Vienna

Gebrüder Pfeiffer
Köppelsdorf, Germany

Emil Pfeiffer was founded in 1873 and registered its **piper** trademark for composition dolls in 1904 (the word "Pfeiffer" means "piper" in German). The entwined EP mark was used beginning in 1916 and among the trade names registered were **Fritz** (1917), **Hanka** (1924), **Huberta** (1917), and **Hubsy** (1925). **Tipple Topple** (1922) was used to designate the firm's special composition material. Pfeiffer used Armand Marseille heads with mold numbers 390, 560a, and 1894, and also used heads by Ernst Heubach. In 1926, the firm was reorganized as Emil Pfeiffer & Sons. Gebrüder Pfeiffer was the German branch of the Viennese company.

Pierotti

Karl Pietsch
Neustadt and Öslau, Germany

Doll factory and exporter; specialized in jointed dolls and babies, 1921-c. 1930.

M. Pintel, Jr.
Paris

Registered a red, white, and blue striped **ribbon** as a trademark for cloth dolls, 1913. (The ribbon was to be used to trim the dolls' clothing.) In the early 1920s, the firm was known as Pintel Fils.

Plass & Rösner
Buchau, Bohemia

Made bisque dolls' heads and bathing dolls, c. 1907-1913. [Bohemia was part of the Austro-Hungarian empire, hence the words **Made in Austria** on the mark.]

Politzer Toy Manufacturing Co.
New York City

Registered a trademark in 1915; the firm was listed as both a manufacturer and distributor of dolls.

Pollak & Hoffmann
Buchau, Bohemia

Produced bisque dolls' heads, 1902-1907.

Porzellanfabrik Günthersfeld
Gehren, Germany

Friedrich Degenring established this factory by 1881; it manufactured dolls' heads during the 1890s.

Porzellanfabrik Mengersgereuth
Mengersgereuth, Germany

Founded in 1908, this factory made dolls' heads c. 1913-1930. Robert Carl became sole owner in 1925, after which time his RC mark was used by Mengersgereuth, along with variants such as the letters R or X within a circle. Carl designed heads marked **Trebor** ("Robert" backwards). Character dolls named **Grete** and **Herzi** were made; these and others were marked **PM**—initials incorrectly attributed to the Porzellanfabrik Moschendorf of Otto Reinecke until positively identified by the Ciesliks. Mengersgereuth supplied heads to Gebrüder Ohlhaver and Carl Harmus (the triangular trademark was used for these firms; the circular ones for some of the factory's own heads). Known mold numbers include 255, 800, 828, 830, 904, 914, 916, 924, 926, 927, 928, 929, and 950.

Germany

Porzellanfabrik Rauenstein
Rauenstein, Germany

Founded in 1783, this factory began producing dolls' heads and nanking dolls in the 1880s and continued until at least 1930. Mold numbers identified are 114 and 191 (**Alice**), made before 1890 and in 1892, respectively. Letters appearing on incised marks are **A, C, N, P,** and **R,** usually in conjunction with the crossed penants or a mold number. The firm is also known to have produced a bisque head incised **Dora.**

114 ¹²/₀ $\mathcal{N}$

$R = n$

$\mathcal{A}$ lice

$\mathcal{N}$ₒ 191

¹⁴/₀ $\mathcal{A}$

Porzellanfabrik von Alt
(see Alt, Beck & Gottschalck)

Leo Potter
New York City

Registered the trademark **Nockwood** in 1915.

Francisque Poulbot
Paris

Madame Poulbot
Paris

It is not yet known whether Francisque Poulbot and Madame Poulbot are two separate people or one and the same person. Francisque Poulbot registered the trademarks **Un Poulbot** and **Une Poulbotte** in 1913; the Poulbot name is also found on an S.F.B.J. doll (see mark). A Madame Poulbot registered the trademarks illustrated in 1918.

ANSONNET

BABA

COCO

COCO
L'Infernal brise-tout

FANFOIS

Le Petit LARDON

LILI

MOMO

MOUTCHOU

MOUTCHOU
La Mouche

NENETTE

NINI

NINI
La Princesse

PILEFER

RINTINTIN

SAC de TERRE

ZIZINE

S.F.B.J
239
PARIS
Boulbot

William H. Price, Jr.
Akron, Ohio

Registered a trademark for a dancing doll, 1921.

Progressive Toy Co.
New York City

Manufactured composition dolls, some with bisque heads. Among the trade names used were **Admiration** (1917), **Admiration Babies** (1918), **Chatterbox** (1923), **Dimples** (1921), **Eversweets** (1921), **Little Love Pirate** (1919), **Sweetie** (1919), and **Sweetness** (1919).

Adolf Prouza
Klein Schwadowitz-Eipel, Bohemia

Produced bathing dolls and jointed dolls from 1908 until at least 1930.

A.P
1903
8

Wenzel Prouza
Sataliz, Bohemia

Founded in 1905. Made porcelain dolls and bathing dolls through at least 1930.

1899
WEP
3

Puppen-Industrie Gotha
Gotha, Germany

Manufactured doll bodies; registered its **Pigo** trademark in 1924.

Grace Storey Putnam
Oakland, California

Mrs. Putnam, a watercolorist, was an art teacher in Oakland, California. In the early 1920s, she created a doll in imitation of a three-day-old baby, and the result, the **Bye-Lo Baby** (1922), became an astounding commercial success under the expert marketing of George Borgfeldt. Known as the "Million Dollar Baby" because of its enormous sales, the Bye-Lo was first produced with a bisque socket head on a composition body. Within a year, it was offered with a bisque flange neck on a cloth body designed by Mrs. Putnam herself. The bisque heads were made by a number of German manufacturers, including Hertel, Schwab & Co., Kestner, and Kling. All-bisque dolls were made by Kestner; celluloids by Karl Standfuss (starting in 1925). Bye-Los were made of composition as early as 1924 by the Cameo Doll Company and of wood in 1925 by Schoenhut. Mrs. Putnam was under contract to Borgfeldt for at least twenty years and designed several other dolls (marked on the heads, **Copr. by//Grace S Putnam//Germany//**[or **MADE IN GERMANY**]). Some included a mold number as well. The circular mark shown here was used as a label (K & K Toy Company assembled the dolls for Borgfeldt); the mark which includes the number 20-10 was incised on an all-bisque Bye-Lo (probably made by Kestner).

©1923 *by*
Grace S. Putnam
MADE IN GERMANY

20-10
Copr. by
Grace S. Putnam
Germany

Quaker Doll Co.
Philadelphia

Manufactured character dolls under the

trade name **Quaker Quality**, 1915-1918.

R

Rabery & Delphieu
Paris

Founded in 1856, Rabery & Delphieu made cloth, kid-bodied, and jointed dolls, some with bisque heads. After 1890, the initials **R.D.** were used both for composition bébés and for talking dolls. Among the company's trade names were **Bébé Rabery** and **Bébé de Paris** (introduced in 1898). Rabery & Delphieu joined S.F.B.J. in 1899.

R·3·D

Max Rader
Sonneberg, Germany

Made character dolls' heads of bisque and

composition, c. 1910-1913. Known mold numbers include 40, 47, 50, and 5050.

40
R. DEP.
10

S
R 47-6 DEP

Jessie McCutcheon Raleigh
Chicago

Made composition dolls and cloth dolls— many distributed by Butler Bros.—from 1916 to 1920. Among the trade names were:

Baby Petite (1916)
Baby Sister (1919)
Baby Stuart (1919)
Betty Bonnet (1918)

Big Mary (1919)
Bobbie Burns Lassie (1918)
Bye Bye Baby (1918)
Comfort (1920—a cloth doll)
Curly Locks (1916)
Daisy Anna (1919)
Dearie (1916)
Debutante (1918)
Doll-O²-My-Heart (1919)
Dorothy (1919)
Elise (1919)
Evelyn (1919)
Goldilocks (1919)
Helen (1919)
Honey Bunch (1918)
Jane (1916)
Johnny Jump-Up (1918)
Kiddie Kar Kiddie (1916)
Kindergarten Girlie (1918)
Little Brother (1918)
Little Lucille (1919)
Little Miss Happy (1919)
Little Playmate (1918)
Little Princess (1918)
Little Sherry (1919)
Lucille (1919)
Mama's Angel Child (1919)
Mammy Jinny (1920)
Marjorie (1918)
Mary Had a Lamb (1919)
Mary-Quite-Contrary (1919)
Miss Happy (1919)
Miss Sunshine (1918)
Miss Traveler (1916)
Mother's Darling (1918)
My Favorite (1916)
Nancy C. (1918)
Peeps (1918)
Pink Lady (1919)
Polly (1918)
Poppy (1919)
Priscilla (1919)
Rabbit Lady (1919)
Red Riding Hood (1919)
Rosemary (1919)
Sam (1920—a rag doll)
School Girl (1918)
Shoe Button Sue (1920—a rag doll)
Sonie (1918)
Stair-Step Family (1920)
Summer Girl (1918)
Sweetheart (1919)
Tiny Tot (1919)

Uncle Sam (1917)
Vacation Girl (1918)
Winter Girl (1918)

Bernard Ravca
Paris

A famous maker of cloth art dolls during the 1930s and '40s, Ravca gained early popularity with dolls made to represent the entertainers **Maurice Chevalier** and **Mistinguette** (c. 1925). Originally, Ravca's dolls wore paper tags similar to the one shown here; such tags are easily lost, however, and the artist had many imitators.

Louis Reber
Sonneberg, Germany

Founded in 1910; produced leather and rubber dolls, ball-jointed dolls, and character babies through the late 1920s. The mark shown was found on a rubber socket head, c. 1924.

D. R. G. M.
897388
1046

Theodor Recknagel
Alexandrienthal, Germany

Produced bisque heads from c. 1893 to c. 1930; added composition heads after World War I. Note that the initials **RA** (for Recknagel Alexandrienthal) were sometimes reversed to **AR** in the incised marks used by the company. Among the known mold numbers are 22, 28, 31, 39, 47, 86, 121, 126, 127, and 1909. The initials **JK, NG,** or **NK** appear occasionally above the reversed **AR** mark, although their significance is yet unknown.

   1909
DEP

R IX· 11/o   R ''/o A

GERMANÿ
NK4
A. 1. R.

Regal Doll Manufacturing Co.
New York City

Made composition and stuffed dolls, 1918-c. 1928. Among the trade names registered in 1925 were **Hug Me**, **"Kiddie Pal Dolly"**, and **Queen of Toyland**. The company's predecessor was known as German American Doll Co.

Rehbock and Loewenthal
Fürth, Germany

Registered **Chérie Bébé** as a trademark in France, 1914.

CHÉRI BÉBÉ

Ernst Reinhardt
Philadelphia; East Liverpool, Ohio; and Irvington, Metuchen, and Perth Amboy, New Jersey

In 1909, Reinhardt emigrated to America from Germany, where he had briefly operated a doll assembly plant. In Philadelphia, where he first settled, Reinhardt produced bisque-headed dolls with papier-mâché bodies and wooden limbs. In 1917,

he established the short-lived Bisc Novelty Manufacturing Company in Ohio. Between 1918 and 1922, Reinhardt was manufacturing bisque dolls in several New Jersey locations [dolls marked **Perth Amboy** and **Mesa** were made during this time, as was **Augusta** (1920)]. Where Reinhardt was located when the marks shown were used is not known. See also Bisc Novelty Manufacturing Company.

        USA
ER

Reliable Toy Co.
Toronto, Canada

Beginning in 1920, Reliable made composition dolls, generally marked as shown on the head or shoulder plate. Among the trade names advertised before 1940 were **Baby Bunting** (1939), **Peggy** (1939), **Shirley Temple** (1930s), and **Wetums** (1930s). In the 1920s, the company offered a mounty, marked **Reliable/Made in/Canada** on the head, and **R.C.M.P.** on the uniform's epaulets. The firm is still in business today.

RELIABLE
MADE IN CANADA

Frédéric Remignard
Paris

Made dolls and *bébés incassables*, 1884-1890, including **Le Petit Chérubin** (1888).

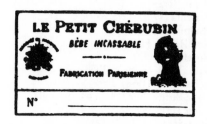

Rémond & Perreau
(see François Guillard)

Moritz Resek
Smichow, Bohemia

Founded in 1889; produced doll parts, bisque heads, and jointed dolls until at least 1920.

$\mathcal{M}$o$\mathcal{R}$o
1895
175
16 ¾

Paul Revere Pottery
Boston and Brighton, Massachusetts

This Massachusetts firm made bisque socket heads and all-bisque dolls during World War I, but abandoned the undertaking when the Germans began to export dolls again in the 1920s. In addition to its initials, P.R.P., the company used marks indicating its decorators, among them BI, C2, and LRT.

P·R·P
110·2

Rheinische Gummi- und Celluloid-Fabrik
Mannheim-Neckarau, Germany

Rheinische Gummi, a rubber-goods factory which eventually became the primary German manufacturer of celluloid dolls, was founded in 1873 and began to use its famous turtle mark (or, in German, Schildkröte) in 1889, though its first dolls weren't produced until 1896. In addition to manufacturing many of its own dolls, it supplied heads—both finished and unfinished—to other major companies, including Buschow & Beck, Kämmer & Reinhardt, Kestner, and König & Wernicke. Many dolls' heads are therefore found with both the turtle mark and another company's mark as well. Registered design patents, or GMs, can sometimes help to date a Rheinische Gummi

doll, but the GM number, which sometimes appeared with the turtle mark, must be matched with the particular doll on which it appears, as many of the numbers were used more than once. For example, GM 12 was registered for a doll in a clown costume (1907), the head of a boy (1910), a dolly head (1912), and a character doll named **Putzi** (1924), among other designs. In 1926, the company registered the trademark **Miblu** to denote its new celluloid, which had a translucent, wax-like appearance. Among the trade names Rheinische Gummi introduced were **Anneliese** (1926), **Hansel** (1930), **Jeff** (1914), **Max** and **Moritz** (1910), **Martha** (1927), **Michel** (1909), **Putzi** (1924), **Rudy** (1926), and **Ruth** (1926).

August Riedeler
Königsee and Garsitz, Germany

Founded in 1864, the Riedeler porcelain factory began to make bisque dolls and dolls' heads in 1872 and within twenty years had expanded production to include nanking bodies, cloth dolls, and dressed bathing dolls. By 1930, the factory was offering celluloid dolls as well, and at one point supplied a million small bisque dolls per year to Woolworth's. Two Riedeler trademarks are shown, along with an incised mark found on a shoulderhead. Among known mold numbers are 6 and 969.

AR
6

Marie Georgette Rigot
Paris

Registered **L'Idéale** as a trademark in 1928.

L'IDÉALE

Maison Rohmer
Paris

From c. 1859 to 1880, sold dolls of kid, cloth, and gutta-percha. The mark shown appeared on kid bodies.

Rookwood Pottery
Cincinnati

This famous pottery firm, founded in 1880, made bisque dolls' heads in the absence of European ones during World War I.

Charles Rossignol
Paris

Made mechanical dolls, 1878-1900.

CR

Henri Rostal
Paris

In 1914, registered **Mon Trésor** and **Bébé**

Mon Trésor as trade names for dolls. Used the initials **HR** as a mark.

MON TRÉSOR

Sigmund I. Rothschild
New York City

Rothschild's trademark, registered in 1919, was printed on a paper label affixed to his dolls.

Roullet & Decamps
Paris

One of the foremost makers of mechanical dolls (acrobats, tambourine players, and magicians, to name a few), Roullet & Decamps was founded in 1865. "L'Intrépide Bébé" was registered as a trademark in 1893; the firm used the initials **RD** as a mark. Its mechanical swimming dolls were known as **Ondine;** Simon & Halbig made the heads.

R.D.

"L'INTRÉPIDE BÉBÉ„

Royal Copenhagen Manufactory
Copenhagen, Denmark

Made china heads with molded hair, c. 1844-1884.

Royal Toy Manufacturing Co.
New York City

Founded in 1914; manufactured the Royal

Doll line which included **Prize Winner Baby** (1924) and **Royal Baby Bunting** (1925).

Edmée Rozier
(see Cecile Lambert)

S

Saalfield Publishing Co.
Akron, Ohio

In 1907, Saalfield introduced its first set of cut-out muslin doll patterns, with characters based on the illustrations of the popular artist Kate Greenaway. Its greatest success, however, was in obtaining exclusive rights to produce **Shirley Temple** paper dolls in the 1930s. Among the rag doll characters Saalfield offered were:

Aunt Dinah (1908)
Baby Blue Eyes (1909)
Delft Girl (1908)
Dolly Dear (1918)
Dottie Dimple (1909)
Fritz (1914)
Goldenlocks (1909)
Little Red Riding Hood (1908)
Papoose (1908)
Santa Claus (1908)

Arthur Sadin
Paris

Registered the trademark **Favori-Bébé** in 1916.

FAVORI = BÉBÉ

Louis Sametz
New York City

Made celluloid dolls, 1918-1924. The company's **Indian-head** mark appeared as a raised insignia on the dolls' backs. Made celluloid **Kewpies** and **Bye-Lo babies**, as well.

Samstag & Hilder Brothers
New York City

Samstag & Hilder, which manufactured and imported dolls from 1894 to 1920, had branches throughout America and Europe, and sold dolls made by many leading German manufacturers, among them Gebrüder Heubach and Steiff. Edmund Steiner became the head of Samstag's doll department after leaving Strobel & Wilken c. 1903; he produced a number of dolls for his new employer, including **Human Face**

Doll, **Liliput**, and **Majestic**. Among the other dolls the firm distributed were:

Baby Cuddles (1920)
Colonial Doll (1905)
Colonial Quality Dolls (1920)
Daisy (1905)
Double Face Dolls (1912)
Duchess (1903)
Featherweight Babies (1913)
Goggle Eye Dolls (1912)
Hug Me Kiddies (1912)
Hooligans (1908)
Katzenjammer (1908)
My Little Beauty (1903)
Our Daisy (1903)
Parcel Post Babies (1913)
Peter Pan Play Dolls (1907)
Royal (1903)
Whistling Jim (1914)

William Webb Sanders
Chateaudun, France

Registered a trademark for dolls, 1927.

Santy
London

The exceptionally rare marked dolls from this firm, c. 1860, have wax-over-composition heads and stuffed bodies.

Johannes Sauerteig
Sonneberg, Germany

Founded in 1864; produced talking dolls,

jointed dolls, and doll bodies, c. 1879 to c. 1924.

Enrico Scavini
(see Lenci)

Otto Schamberger
Sonneberg, Germany

Used the trademark **Adlon** for dolls, c. 1923-1925. Probably ordered heads from other firms.

Max Friedrich Schelhorn
Sonneberg, Germany

Made dolls and doll parts, 1907-c.1925. Among the trade names of its dolls were **The Base Ball Fan** (1914), **Fluffy Ruffles** (1907), **Little Snookums** (1910), **Muffles** (1910), **The Newlywed's Baby** (1910), and **Peter Pan Playtoys** (1907). Its mark was based on a trademark registered in 1908.

August Schellhorn
Sonneberg, Germany

Founded in 1887; produced dolls until at least 1932.

Peter Scherf
Sonneberg, Germany

Founded c. 1879; made poured wax dolls

and later bisque-headed dolls, (some with heads supplied by Armand Marseille). Exported many of its inexpensive dolls to the United States during the early 20th century, including character dolls. Registered **The Fairy Kid** (1916) as a trade name.

Scheyer & Co.
Nuremberg, Sonneberg, and Olbernhau, Germany

Registered **Floresta** (1920) and **Mafuka** (1925) as trademarks for dolls.

F. M. Schilling
Sonneberg, Germany

Founded in 1871; produced papier-mâché, rubber, composition, and wax dolls until the 1920s. Registered the trademark **Biskuit-Facon** (bisque model) to protect its special, durable papier-mâché material in 1878; the **angel** trademark was registered a year later.

Titus Schindel & Co.
(see Wiesenthal, Schindel & Kallenberg)

Mme. Jeanne Schlisler
Paris

Registered **Ti-Koun** as a trademark for dolls, 1924.

TI-KOUN

Albert Schlopsnies
(see Bing Kunstlerpuppen- und Stoffspielwarengesellschaft)

Bruno Schmidt
Waltershausen, Germany

Founded in 1900, the Bruno Schmidt factory made dolls and babies of celluloid and of wood. Its **Herz** (**heart**) trademark with the initials **BSW** was registered in 1904; the heart alone was registered in 1908. Schmidt offered many character babies during the early 20th century; many had bisque heads purchased exclusively from Bähr & Pröschild, whose factory was purchased by Schmidt in 1918. [**Mein Goldherz** (My Golden Heart) was used as a trade name for character babies beginning in 1910.] Because of the closeness of the two firms' relationship, the Bähr & Pröschild bisque heads often bear both firms' trademarks (heart and **crossed swords**) as well as two sets of mold numbers. Three-digit numbers were Bähr & Pröschild's; four-digit, Schmidt's. Among the known mold numbers used by Bruno Schmidt were 2023, 2025, 2048, 2068, 2070, 2074, 2075, 2081, 2084, 2085, 2092, 2094, 2095, 2096, 2097, 2098, and 2154. Celluloid heads made at the Schmidt factory after 1919 include the letter S or G with the heart trademark.

Franz Schmidt & Co.
Georgenthal, Germany

Franz Schmidt founded his doll factory in 1890 and was soon offering many types of dolls, including models in wood, leather, composition, and bisque. (All of its bisque heads were made by Simon & Halbig, using Schmidt's designs.) Schmidt was famed as an innovator and is credited with a number of inventions and improvements to the character doll, including sleeping eyes, pierced nostrils (1912), and movable tongues (1913). The Schmidt company registered several trademarks, among them FS & C with a doll flanked by crossed hammers (1902) and Cellobrin (1909), denoting dolls' heads and other parts made of a special material produced in one of its plants. The mark S & C was used before 1902 and the anvil mark was used prior to 1900. The three circular marks shown were used as stamps on dolls' bodies.

Among the mold numbers used on Schmidt heads were 269, 293, 927, 1180, 1250, 1253, 1259, 1262, 1263, 1266, 1267, 1270, 1271, 1272, 1274, 1293, 1295, 1296, 1297, 1298, 1299, 1310, and 1409. Bisque heads made by Simon & Halbig for Schmidt carried mold numbers 1180, 1293, 1295 through 1299, and 1310. The small Z which often appears in conjunction with the mold number and a size number stands for *Zentimeter,* German for "centimeter." The Franz Schmidt factory made dolls until 1945.

1296

F.S.& C.

SIMON & HALBIG

Made in

Germany

Germany

S&C 1180-13

F. S. & C.

1272/40 Z

Deponiert

F.S & C°

1271/32 Z

Deponiert

Paul Schmidt
Sonneberg, Germany

Advertised dolls and toys with the trademark PESO in 1922; registered the circular PSSTh trademark in the same year and the simpler PS trademark a year later.

S&C

SIMON & HALBIG

28

4536

Schmitt & Fils
Paris

Produced **Bébé Schmitt,** a jointed indestructible baby with a bisque head, 1879-1890. Note the similarity of the **crossed hammer** mark used by Schmitt on dolls' heads and bodies to the 1902 label of Germany's Franz Schmidt.

P. H. Schmitz
Paris

A maker of dolls and bébés, Schmitz joined S.F.B.J. in 1903, after ten years of independent work. His trademark **Bébé Moderne** was first registered in 1893 and then renewed by S.F.B.J. in 1903.

Heinrich Schmuckler
Liegnitz, Germany

Founded in 1882, the firm produced woolen, celluloid, and rubber dolls until c. 1928. The trademark **Hesli,** used for dressed dolls, was registered in 1921.

[Schmuckler's factory was known as Erste Schleisische Puppenfabrik (the first Silesia doll factory), though the Hesli trademark is obviously an abbreviation of Heinrich Schmuckler, Liegnitz.]

Schneider
Paris

Manufactured jointed dolls, and cloth and kid-bodied dolls, some with bisque heads, 1858-1896. Registered **S.F.** as a trademark in 1888, three years after the firm's name was changed from Schneider to Schneider Fils.

Carl Schneider, Erben
Gräfenthal, Germany

Porcelain factory founded as Unger, Schneider and Hutschenreuther in 1861; by 1886, it was named Carl Schneider, Erben (Carl Schneider's heirs). Its trademark, registered in 1894, was used on bathing dolls. The porcelain factory was in operation through the 1960s.

Robert Schneider
Coburg, Germany

Registered **Roschco** as a trademark, 1924.

Schoen & Yondorf
New York City

Made a variety of composition and rag dolls during the first quarter of the 20th century, including **Creeping Baby** (1925), **Dancing Katharina** (1925), **Hell'n Maria** (**Miss Helen Maria**) (1924), **Mistah Sunshine** (1923), **My Bunny Boy** (1923), **Our Gang dolls** (1925), and **Teddy in Boots** (1923). All were advertised under the trade name **Sayco**.

Arthur Schoenau
Sonneberg, Germany

Arthur Schoenau bought an existing doll factory in Sonneberg in 1884 and launched a separate porcelain factory in Burggrub in 1901 (see Schoenau & Hoffmeister). In its early years, the Sonneberg factory ordered bisque heads from Simon & Halbig, Gebrüder Kuhnlenz, Th. Recknagel, Bähr & Pröschild, and other German makers. The later heads were supplied by its own factory in Burggrub; thus the marks of Schoenau and of Schoenau & Hoffmeister are often similar, if not identical, making positive identification difficult. About the only marks that can be definitely attributed to Schoenau in Sonneberg rather than to the Burggrub factory are the founder's **AS** or **ASS** initials. Among the jointed dolls and babies Schoenau offered were **Bébé Carmencita** (1913), **Carmencita** (1912), **Hanna** (1910), **My Cherub** (1912), **Princess Elizabeth** (c. 1937), and **Prinzessin Wunderhold** (1912). [The **M.B.** in one of the incised marks shown stands for the first and last letters of Mein Cherub.]

M.B.
Germany
500

Schoenau & Hoffmeister
Burggrub, Germany

Founded by Arthur Schoenau and his partner Carl Hoffmeister in 1901, this porcelain factory supplied bisque heads to Schoenau's Sonneberg company and to many other firms as well, including Canzler & Hoffman, Cuno & Otto Dressel, and Ernst Maar. Because of the close relationship between the two Schoenau factories, many of their marks are similar and the trade names overlap as well. Schoenau & Hoffmeister heads marked **Das lachende Baby, Hanna, Künstlerkopf, My Cherub, Princess Elizabeth,** and **Viola** have been identified. In addition, Schoenau & Hoffmeister used the following mold numbers (in conjunction with the letters **SHPB** and a **five-pointed star**) before 1930: 900, 914, 1400, 1800, 1904, 1906, 1909, 1930, 2500, 4000, 4001, 4500, 4600, 4700, 4900, 5000, 5300, 5500, 5700, and 5800. Dolls made after 1930 were incised **Porzellanfabrik Burggrub** together with the number 169 or 170 and sometimes the word **Spezial**. Initials other than SHPB were also used, among them **DALABA** (for Das lachende Baby), **MB** (My Cherub), and **NKB** and **WSB** (found together with the star and SHPB on the head of a character baby). The Schoenau & Hoffmeister factory produced heads until c. 1953.

Porzellanfabrik
Burggrub

Das lachende Baby
1930-2

Made in Germany

D.R.G.M.

Hanna
2

A. Schoenhut & Co.
Philadelphia

Albert Schoenhut was a descendant of German woodcarvers and emigrated to the United States at the age of 17. Within just five years (by 1872) he had founded his own company. For its first few decades, Schoenhut chiefly made musical toys (including the first toy pianos), but just after the turn of the century began to produce wooden dolls as well. In 1903, the company patented the first figures in its **Humpty Dumpty Circus**, a group of circus performers including a lion tamer, ringmaster, and lady acrobat. All were identical except for the clothes and paint. Schoenhut made both jointed dolls and bent-limb babies; until 1924, the dolls were all of wood. In that year the firm introduced cloth-bodied dolls with wooden heads and used composition for some of its dolls after 1928.

The circular mark shown was incised on the backs of dolls' heads and also used as a decal; the larger elliptical mark was used as a decal on bodies. In some cases, the company incised the following on dolls' bodies: SCHOENHUT DOLL//PAT. JAN. 17, '11, U.S.A. // & FOREIGN COUNTRIES. A line of dolls called **All**

Wood Perfection Art Dolls was introduced in 1911. Each doll was sold with a circular tin pin attached. Within a shield at its center were the words SCHOENHUT// ALL WOOD//PERFECTION ART DOLL; around the outside a tag line read MADE IN U.S.A. STRONG, DURABLE AND UNBREAKABLE. In 1913, Schoenhut introduced a line of dolls under the name **Baby's Head**; a later group of dolls was called **Miss Dolly Schoenhut** (1915). The company made a very few wooden infants resembling the popular **Bye-Lo** in 1925. Schoenhut went into bankruptcy during the Great Depression.

Among the names given to individual Schoenhut dolls prior to 1911 (after which they were assigned numbers for ordering purposes, though the numbers did not appear on the dolls) were:

Chinaman Acrobat (1906)
Clown (1903)
Farmer (1908)
Gent Acrobat (c. 1905)
Hobo (c. 1904)
Milk Maid (1908)
Mr. Common People (1911)
Miss Dolly Schoenhut (1915)
Moritz (1907)
Negro Dude (c. 1904)
Ring Master (c. 1905)
Schnickel-Fritz (1911)
Teddy Roosevelt (c. 1909)
Tootsie-Wootsie (1911)

Schreyer & Co.
Nuremberg, Germany

Founded in 1923, this firm made cloth character dolls, which were distributed by Borgfeldt and Louis Wolf. It used the trademark **Shuco**.

Schützmeister & Quendt
Boilstädt, Germany

Founded in 1889, this porcelain factory produced bisque dolls and dolls' heads, jointed dolls, and cloth dolls. After 1918 its dolls' heads were made only for Kämmer & Reinhardt and Welsch & Co., by then members of a holding company called Concentra, which Schützmeister & Quendt also joined. The firm's intertwined SQ trademark is incised on heads, along with a mold number. Among the known mold numbers are 101, 102, 201, 204, 252, 300, 301, and 1376. The factory continued to manufacture tea-cozy dolls, porcelain dolls, and dolls' heads until c. 1930.

Sig. Schwartz Co.
New York City

Made dolls, 1917-1922. Used the trade

names Joy Toies (1920), Tynie-Tots (1917), and **Water Babies** (1919).

Sigismund Schwerin
Breslau, Germany

Founded in 1884; registered **SSN** (1923) and **Hedi** (1924) as trademarks for its dolls.

Seamless Toy Corp.
New York City

Founded in 1918; manufactured wood-fiber composition dolls. Among its trade names were **American Beauty** (1919), **Kutie Kid** (1920), **Pretty Polly** (1919), and **Willie Walker** (1920).

Sears, Roebuck & Co.
Chicago

The famous mail-order house, founded in 1888, imported and distributed dolls, including several exclusive lines. Among the trade names it handled were:

American Maid (1910)
Baby Ruth (1914)
Baby Sunshine (1925—see mark)
Dainty Dorothy (1910—see mark)
Feather Light Brand (c. 1914)
Knockout Grade (1893)
Pansy Kid (1914—see mark)
Playmates (1922)
Sunshine (1913)
Violet (1910)
Wearwell Brand (1922)

SUNSHINE

PANSY
IV
Germany

Eugène Sedard
Sceaux, France

Made wooden dolls, 1919.

Seigenberg & Sher
Los Angeles

Registered a trademark for dolls in 1923; indicated that it was to be used on a printed label.

Selchow & Righter
New York City

From 1883 to 1923, this toy distributor sold

dolls from various companies, including Arnold Print Works and Art Fabric Mills, which it took over in 1911. During the second decade of the twentieth century, the company advertised imported dolls and it used the initials **S & R** in the early '20s.

Seligman & Braun
Hoboken, New Jersey

Between 1911 and 1913, this firm made unbreakable dolls and talking stuffed dolls. Among the trade names were **Bridget** (1911), **Gloom** (1912), **Joy** (1911) **Mike** (1911), **School Boy** (1911), and **School Girl** (1911).

Seligmann & Mayer
Sonneberg, Germany

Registered **Mi Encanto** as a trademark for dolls in 1930.

Seyfarth & Reinhardt
Waltershausen, Germany

The partnership of Seyfarth & Reinhardt was formed in 1922 and registered **Elfe** and **My Fairy** as trademarks in its first year. **SUR** was registered in 1923. The factory made jointed dolls, bent-limb babies, and doll parts until the 1930s. As the mark shows, Seyfarth & Reinhardt used bisque heads by Ernst Heubach for some of its dolls.

Heubach - Köppelsdorf
312 (SuR) 6½
Germany.

Elsie Shaver
New York City

Registered the trademark **Little Shavers** for cloth dolls in 1919. It was to be used on a printed label attached to the doll. A second trademark, also registered in 1919, was **Olie-ke-Wob**. It was intended to be stamped on the package.

Lita and Bessie Shinn
Muskogee, Oklahoma

Made hand-painted rag dolls stuffed with cotton, 1916-1920. The mark shown sometimes appeared on the sole of the foot.

Shulman & Sons
New York City

Imported and sold rubber dolls and bisque-headed dolls, 1906-1924. In addition to the mark shown, used the advertising slogan **The House of Service.**

Simon & Halbig
Gräfenhain, Germany

After Armand Marseille, the firm of Simon & Halbig was the second largest maker of dolls' heads in Germany. The company originated in 1869 as a porcelain factory, but since its co-founder, Wilhelm Simon, was also a toy manufacturer who produced dolls, the new firm took advantage of the growing vogue for bisque-headed dolls by producing dolls' heads, both for its own use and for other companies as well. For this reason, Simon & Halbig's shoulderheads are among the earliest marked bisques available to collectors, though precise dating is difficult as many of the molds, carrying the same numbers throughout their "life cycles," were produced in various sizes over several decades or more and were sometimes used both on Simon & Halbig dolls and on heads destined for other factories.

Simon & Halbig produced bisque heads for many other European manufacturers; after 1902, it supplied all of Kämmer & Reinhardt's bisque heads, a dependence that no doubt led to K & R's acquisition of the S & H firm in 1920. Among the many other companies for which Simon & Halbig supplied heads were C. M. Bergmann, Carl Bergner, Cuno & Otto Dressel, R. Eeckhoff, Fleischmann & Bloedel, Hamburger & Co., Heinrich Handwerck, Adolf Hülss, Jumeau, Louis Lindner, Roullet & Decamps, Franz Schmidt, S.F.B.J., Carl Trautmann, Welsch & Co., Hugo Wiegand, Wiesenthal Schindel & Kallenberg, and Adolf Wislizenus. Specific mold numbers reserved exclusively for those companies, along with trade names which sometimes appeared as part of the marks, can be found in the individual company listings.

Of the marks shown here, the **seated Chinese** is the earliest; it was registered as a trademark for packaging materials in 1875. The inclusion of **DEP** in the mark indicates that the doll was made after 1887. The famous **S & H** mark first used the ampersand in 1905; **SH** marks without the ampersand are consequently thought to date before 1905. Simon & Halbig's successor, Keramisches Werk Gräfenhain, used the **KWG** mark after 1930.

Mold numbers and marks used by the Gräfenhain factory are generally incised on one of three places: on the back of the head, the back of the shoulder plate, or the front of the shoulder plate. Among the mold numbers the factory used for its own dolls were 120, 122P, 150, 151, 152, 153, 170 through 175 inclusive, 305, 332 through 344 inclusive, 351 through 370 inclusive, 415 through 435 inclusive, 500, 516, 530, 540, 550, 570, 600, 607, 610, 611, 616, 620, 693, 719, 720, 728, 729, 738, 739, 740, 748, 749, 750, 758, 759, 768, 769, 778, 837, 845, 846, 847, 848, 852, 878, 880, 881, 886, 887, 890, 896, 898, 899, 905, 908, 909, 918, 919, 920, 921, 927, 929, 939, 940, 941 949, 950, 959, 968, 969, 970, 979, 989, 1000, 1008, 1009, 1010, 1018, 1019, 1029, 1038, 1039, 1040, 1041, 1049, 1058, 1059, 1060, 1061, 1068, 1069, 1078, 1079, 1080, 1098, 1099, 1108, 1109, 1129, 1139, 1148, 1150, 1158, 1159, 1160, 1170, 1180, 1199, 1246, 1248, 1249, 1250, 1260, 1269, 1278, 1279, 1280, 1289, 1294, 1300 through 1305 inclusive, 1307, 1308, 1329, 1340, 1358, 1368, 1370, 1388, 1397, 1398, 1426, 1428, 1448, 1465, 1478, 1485, 1488, 1489, 1496, 1498, 1527, 1616, 1748, and 1916.

Mold numbers included here are only those which have been positively identified as having been used by Simon & Halbig. In their *German Doll Encyclopedia*, Jürgen and Marianne Cieslik have shed much welcome light on Simon & Halbig's numbering system. They discovered that some series of numbers, beginning with final digit 8 in the number and following in numerical order thereafter, were reserved for different versions of the same mold. For example, one of S & H's most popular molds, a dolly-faced doll, has been found with the numbers 1078 (most likely the first, or "test", version of the design), 1079 (a socket head), and 1080 (a shoulder-head); it was probably made as a shoulder plate (1081) as well. Some series of numbers seem to have been reserved for specific types of dolls: the 400 series was used for porcelain figures, the 800 series for small all-bisque dolls and bathing dolls.

S15H 719 DEP

S3H 949
886 S12H

S.H. 1039
Germany
DEP
10½

S & H 1079
DEP
Germany
15

SH 1080 DEP 7

1358
Germany
SIMON & HALBIG

S&H
5

K.W.
G.

In die Masse gestempelt.   Auf den Etiketten.

F. Simonne
Paris

The mark of Simonne, a maker of kid-bodied dolls between 1863 and 1878, is found in turquoise on the stomachs of some dolls.

Edward Smith
London

Sold wax dolls in the 1880s; his mark appeared on the dolls' bodies.

Ella Smith
Roanoake, Alabama

Made the **Alabama Indestructible Doll**, a cloth doll in both black and white models, 1904-1924. Her mark appeared on the bodies.

PAT. NOV.9,1912
NO.2
ELLA SMITH DOLL CO.

Samson Smith
Longton, England

Made china dolls, beginning in 1846. Those made before 1858 bear two **entwined S's**; after that date and well into the 1900s, **Ltd.** was added.

Société Anonyme
Paris

Société Anonyme de Comptoir Generale de la Bimbeloterie
Paris

Because these two firms have similar names and were operating at basically the same time, it is possible that they are, in fact, identical, though there is no evidence either way. Société Anonyme registered **La Parisienne** and **Eureka** as trademarks for dolls c. 1910. Its counterpart registered several **Parisiana** trademarks, as shown, in 1905.

Poupée Parisiana

Bébé Parisiana

Poupon Parisiana

Société au Bébé Rose
Paris

Registered its trademark for dolls, **Au Bébé Rose**, in 1910. The mark was to be printed in violet ink.

Société Binder & Cie.
Paris

Registered its trademark, **B. K.**, for rag dolls in 1918. (The firm was also known as Binder & Cie.)

Société Française de Fabrication de Bébés et Jouets (S.F.B.J.)
Paris and Montreuil-sous-Bois

In 1899, unable to compete successfully with the increasing production and quality of German dolls, most of the struggling French firms signed an agreement to form a syndicate. The original companies to join included Bru, Fleischmann & Bloedel, Jumeau, and Rabery & Delphieu. A few years later Ad. Bouchet and P.H. Schmitz were added, with Danel & Cie. joining in 1911. While the syndicate used some German parts (including Simon & Halbig heads, which it imported from 1900 to 1914), it continued to make heads and bodies in French factories as well. Most S.F.B.J. dolls were bisque-headed bébés on jointed composition bodies.

Although most of the premier French firms were absorbed by the syndicate, the dolls they had introduced earlier continued to be manufactured, so that as late as 1921 Bébé Bru, Bébé Jumeau, and Eden Bébé were still being marketed under their old names. Some of the earlier marks, such as the Jumeau bee, were recycled as well (it was reregistered in 1906). Among the trade names S.F.B.J. registered were **Bébé Français** (1911), **Bébé Jumeau** (1911), **Bébé Moderne** (1920), **Bébé Moderne Le Séduisant** (1903), **Bébé Parfait** (1920), **Bébé Parisiana** (1920), **Bébé Prodige** (1911), **Bébé Triomphe** (1913), **Le Papillon** (1921), **Le Séduisant** (1920), and **Unis France** (1921). The S.F.B.J. trademark was registered in 1905.

FRANCE
SFBJ
301
PARIS
8

25

**BÉBÉ MODERNE
LE SÉDUISANT**

"BÉBÉ PARISIANA"

LE PAPILLON

EDEN-BÉBÉ

PARIS-BÉBÉ

S.F.B.J
236
PARIS

DÉPOSÉ
S.F.B.J.

71   149

251

Société Industrielle de Celluloid
Paris

Made celluloid dolls out of **Sicoid** or Sicoïne, a pyroxylin material, beginning in 1902. The manufacturing firm of Neumann & Marx (1906-1911) was a member of this society; its mark, the **winged dragon with shield** bearing the initials **NM**, was taken over by the society in 1914. Société Industrielle de Celluloid made dolls and babies well into the 1920s. The **Sicoïne** mark shown was raised, rather than incised, on a doll's head.

Société La Parisienne
Paris

Registered the following trademarks for dolls, 1911:

BÉBÉ EUREKA

BÉBÉ FRANÇAIS

BÉBÉ JUMEAU

BÉBÉ LE RÊVE

BÉBÉ PRODIGE

PARADIS BÉBÉ

Société Nobel Française
France

Little is known about this manufacturer of celluloid dolls, save that its trademark, the initials **SNF** within a **diamond**, was first registered in 1939 and the mark was incised both on dolls' heads and on the bodies.

Société Ch. Ramel & Cie.
Paris

Registered two trademarks for papier-mâché dolls in 1916.

J'HABILLE MES POUPÉES

J'HABILLE MES SOLDATS

Société René Schiller & Cie.
Paris

In 1918, registered a trademark for its dolls, which were dressed in the traditional peasant costumes of Alsace and Lorraine.

YERRI et SUZEL

Société Steiner
(see Jules Nicholas Steiner)

Société Sussfeld & Cie.
Paris

Doll distributors; registered two trademarks in 1917.

Sonneberger Porzellanfabrik
Sonneberg, Germany

Founded by Carl Müller in 1883; produced bisque heads from c. 1893 to 1913.

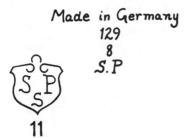

Made in Germany
129
8
S. P

11

Mme. Yvonne Spaggiari
Paris

Registered a trademark for peasant dolls, 1927.

LES ORIGINAUX
DE VOVONNE

Mylius Sperschneider
Sonneberg, Germany

Founded in 1880; made ball-jointed dolls and cloth dolls until about 1927. The firm's **Marionette MSS** trademark was registered in 1921.

Max Spindler & Co.
Köppelsdorf and Sonneberg, Germany

Advertised bisque dolls' heads and dressed dolls in 1920.

Standard Doll Co.
New York City

Made dolls, 1917. Used the trade names **Cadet, French Zouave, Miss America, Scotch Highlander,** and **Uncle Sam.**

Karl Standfuss
Dresden, Germany

Manufactured celluloid and metal dolls and dolls' heads, c. 1898-1930. The **Juno** trademark, first used in 1903, applied to both celluloid and metal dolls. In 1913, Standfuss introduced the trade name **Cupido.** During 1926, the firm advertised that it was the exclusive manufacturer of celluloid **Kewpies** and that it also made celluloid **Bye-Los**.

TRADE MARK

GESCHSCH

Margarete Steiff
Giengen, Germany

Steiff established a felt clothing factory in 1877 and began to make felt dolls in 1893. The earliest trademark, a **camel**, was registered in 1892; the **elephant** in 1905 (though it had been used since 1898); and the circular **KNOPF im OHR**(button in ear) in 1905, introduced in France as **Bouton dans l'oreille** (with the cat-like figure) two years later. The **Steiff** name itself was registered in 1911. Steiff made the first teddy bear, trademarked **Petz**, in 1903, and later changed its name to **Teddy**. The firm also produced a number of character dolls after 1911, many of them designed by Albert Schlopsnies. Among Schlopsnies' designs was a doll called **Aprico** (1921), which was marketed with a red bracelet on which the words **Steiff-//Schlopsnies//Puppe** appeared. Most Steiff dolls made after 1905 have a metal button in the left ear with one of the button-in-ear trademarks. In addition, most can be easily identified by their exaggeratedly large feet, which enable them

to stand unsupported, and by the seam which runs down the center of the faces. Steiff still manufactures dolls and toys today. Among the trade names used for Steiff dolls were:

Alida (1909)
Anthony (1909)
Aprico (1921)
Billy (1909)
Brownie Policeman (1905)
Hubertus (1909)
Kentucky Donkey (1905)
Olaf (1909)
Private Murphy (1909)
Private Sharkey (1909)
Sargent Kelly (1909)

Schutz Marke

Bouton dans l'oreille.

„Steiff"

August Steiner
Köppelsdorf, Germany

Founded in 1900; specialized in composition heads. In business until c. 1930.

A.S
Germany
261/0

A.Steiner-Köppelsdorf
A.S
Germany
84
2/o

Edmund Ulrich Steiner
Sonneberg, Germany and New York City

Steiner, born in Germany, was closely associated with doll manufacturing both in his native country and in the United States during the last quarter of the 19th century and the first fifteen years of the 20th. He worked for a number of firms, including Louis Wolf, Samstag & Hilder, and Strobel & Wilken, and registered several designs for dolls, including a walking doll called **Majestic** and another doll called **Liliput** whose trademarks he registered in 1902, though he had introduced the dolls eight years earlier. **Daisy** was registered as a trademark in Germany in 1903, and in the United States by Samstag & Hilder two years later. Steiner's designs appear to have been manufactured by several companies, including Armand Marseille, as the **Majestic A 8/0 M Made in Germany** mark suggests. Steiner's initials within the diamond were found on a doll made c. 1900.

E.U.St

Made in Germany°½

Majestic
oRegd

MAJESTIC
A 8/0 M
Made in Germany

Hermann Steiner
Neustadt, Germany

Founded in 1920, this porcelain factory produced bisque and, later, composition heads and character babies, and is probably best-known for its exaggerated googlies— dolls with eyes glancing to the side—which were very popular during the early 1900s. Its **My Pearl** trademark was registered in 1921. The Steiner company also made heads for other German firms, including M. Kohnstamm & Co.; Steiner's distinctive entwined initials have been found incised on the head of late versions of Kohnstamm's **Moko**. Among the mold numbers Steiner used were 128, 133, 134, 223, 240, 242, 245, 246, 247, 395, 401, and 1000.

Germany

128
Herm.Steiner
22
0.

H.401 0½ S
Made in Germany

Jules Nicholas Steiner
Paris

Founded in 1855, this firm (also called Société Steiner) specialized in mechanical bébés which walked and talked, and claimed to have invented the bébé. While this is a dubious boast, it is true that Steiner manufactured many early bébés, as well as some of the comeliest ones. A. Lafosse succeeded the company's founder, Jules

Nicholas Steiner, in 1892, and was in turn succeeded by Jules Mettais in 1902 and by E. Daspres in 1906. Because of the firm's various owners, marks can differ greatly. Walking dolls are marked on the actual mechanism; some of the dolls' heads are marked **J. Steiner** or simply **Ste.** The figure of a **doll holding a flag** was registered in 1889 and was used on a label on dolls' bodies; the **Bébé "Le Parisien"** mark appeared as a body stamp after 1892. The **lamp** was used by Jules Mettais after 1902. Some Steiner dolls are marked with the name **Bourgoin** in addition to the firm name; no explanation has been found. Steiner seems to have used letters instead of numbers to indicate molds; dolls have been found with the letters **A, C, D,** and **FA** incised together with one of the Steiner marks. Among the trade names used by the company were:

Baby (1899—see mark)
Bébé Liège (1899—see mark)
Bébé Marcheur (1890)
Bébé Model (1901)
Bébé Phénix (1895)
Bébé Premier Pas (1890)
La Patricienne (1908)
Le Parisien (1892—see marks)
Le Phénix (1899)
Mascotte (1901)
Phénix Bébé (Phénix-Baby) (1899—see mark)
Poupée Merveilleuse (1899—see mark)

STEINER
. S.G.D.G.
PARIS
A II

J. STEINER
Ste S.G.D.G.
PARIS
F I^{ce} A I5

BÉBÉ "LE PARISIEN"
Médaille d'Or
PARIS

MARQUE DE   FABRIQUE

BABY
BÉBÉ-LIÈGE
PHÉNIX-BABY
POUPÉE MERVEILLEUSE

Steinfeld Bros.
New York City

Doll importers and manufacturers, 1898-1917. Made **Racketty Packetty Kiddies** (1913), a series of unbreakable character dolls based on characters from the book of that name by Frances Hodgson Burnett. The dolls were designed by Maurice F. Oppenheimer.

A. Steinhardt & Bros.
New York City

Manufactured a range of **Neverbreak** composition character dolls, 1910-1912, including:

Bess (1910)
Buttons (1911)
Columbine (1911)
Dutch-He and Dutch-She (1911)
Honey Boy (1910)
Jockey (1911)
Marceline (1911)
Mugsey (1911)
Pierrot (1911)
Smiling Sue (1910)
Teddy Jr. (1910)
Twee Deedle (1911)
Wilhewin (1911)

(Teddy Jr. and Smiling Sue had ribbons across their chests bearing their names.)

Abbie B. Stevens
Atlanta, Georgia

Registered her trademark in 1919 for dolls.

Gebrüder Stollwerch
Cologne, Germany

Registered its trademark in 1906 for dolls.

Strasburger, Pfeiffer & Co.
New York City

Between 1851 and 1881, the firm imported, produced, and distributed dolls, including those of New York Rubber Company. The company made and/or sold a wide variety of rubber, bisque, china, wax, kid, and rag dolls. Its trademark, used as a label, was registered in 1871, though it had already been used for two years.

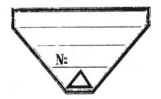

Josef Strasser
Munich, Germany

Made art dolls, c. 1925.

Nur echt mit dieser Schutzmarke!

Adolph Strauss & Co.
New York City

Founded in 1857, Adolph Strauss & Co. probably did not begin importing dolls for distribution until 1912. At first the company used the trade name **Asco** and the slogan shown, **The House of Service.** In 1923, the firm's name was changed to Strauss-Eckhardt Company, the trade name to **Seco,** and the slogan was revised accordingly, though the elliptical mark remained basically the same. (The Seco trademark was renewed in 1937). Among the dolls Strauss sold were mama dolls, **Kidoline** dolls, and character dolls. In 1922, it registered the **Our Pet** trademark in the U.S. for the same doll made by Gebrüder Eckhardt of Sonneberg, Germany (Max Eckhardt was about to become a partner in A. Strauss; his brothers ran the German company). **Our Pet** featured a bisque head made by Armand Marseille. For the mark, see Gebrüder Eckhardt.

Strobel & Wilkin Co.
New York City and Cincinnati, Ohio

From 1849 until the beginning of the Civil War, Strobel & Wilken produced leather goods in Cincinnati. At the war's end, the company turned to importing and distributing dolls, and by 1886 the center of its operation had been moved to New York. Until publication of the Ciesliks' *German Doll Encyclopedia*, a variation of the entwined **SW** trademark shown here had been falsely identified as the company's mark on dolls. The S & W trademark was used only on packaging materials. The nearly identical mark incised on dolls' heads was used by Walther & Sohn of Sonneberg and is pictured under that company's listing. Strobel & Wilken distributed dolls made by a number of German and American firms, including Kämmer & Reinhardt, Hertel, Schwab, & Co., and Ideal Novelty and Toy Company. Among the trade names it advertised were:

Aluminia (1913)
American Beauty (1895)
American Fashion (1905)
Arabesque (1914)
Bertie (1911)
Boy Scout (1916)
Brighto (1914)
Buddy (1916)
Cuddlekins (1917)
Darling (1905)
Diabolo (1908)
Faith (1916)
Gertie (1911)
Hansel (1916)
Jimmy (1916)
Jubilee (1905)
Kanwashem (1905)
Liesel (1916)
Nemo (1914)

Our Pride Kidette (1914)
Peach (1914)
Royal Dolls (1903)
Snow White (1918)
Susie's Sister (1915)
Tootsie (1915)
Ulrich (1916)
Waldorf (1905)
Wonderland (1905)

Wilhelm Strunz
Nuremberg, Germany

Founded in 1902, Strunz manufactured cloth dolls and animals. In 1908, Margarete Steiff took legal action against Strunz, claiming an infringement on her patent of a button in the ear. Thereafter, Strunz agreed to alter his trademark button so that it was affixed to the ear by a wire clamp, rather than being inserted directly in the ear, as Steiff's was.

India King Stubbs
Monroe, Louisiana

Registered **Actoe** as a trademark for dolls, 1923.

Gebrüder Süssenguth
Neustadt, Germany

Founded in 1894, this doll factory specialized in lightweight cloth, leather, and composition dolls for export. It also ordered dolls from other German firms, including Max Oskar Arnold, Cuno & Otto Dressel, and Guttman & Schiffnie. Its trademark was registered in 1904, and the company was known to use the abbreviation **GESUE** as a mark on socket heads.

Puppe der Zukunft

Sussfeld & Cie.
(see Société Sussfeld & Cie.)

Swaine & Co.
Hüttensteinach, Germany

Founded in 1810, this porcelain factory made character dolls' heads for a brief period beginning in 1910. Its **S & Co** mark, found stamped in green on bisque heads (along with **Geschutzt Germany,** as shown here) was a mystery to collectors until

publication of the Ciesliks' *German Doll Encyclopedia.* In addition to the circular stamp, **S & C** was sometimes incised on the head, and the letters **BP, DV, DI, DIP,** and **FP** are also found incised on Swaine heads, though the Ciesliks caution that without the green stamp no positive attribution is possible.

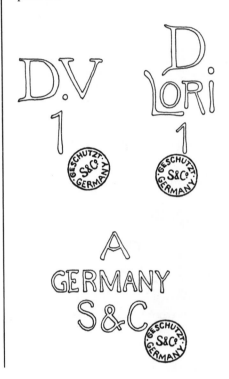

T

Taiyo Trading Co.
New York City and Toronto

Taiyo Trading resulted from the merger of two Japanese import firms in 1919—Tajimi Company and Takito, Ogawa & Company. Among the trade names the new firm advertised were **Baby Lucy** (1919), **Geisha** (1920), and **Ming Toy** (1919). It specialized in importing bisque-headed, jointed dolls.

Tajimi Company (1917-1918) had used the mark shown here.

Terrène
Paris

Made bisque-headed dolls, c. 1867-1890. Bodies were a combination of kid-covered wood, metal (for the upper arms) and bisque (for the lower arms and hands). The mark shown was used as a label affixed to the body.

9 MÉDAILLES
aux Expositions 1867-68-72-73-74
J. TERRÈNE
10 Rue du Marché St Honoré
PARIS

Sylvain Thalheimer & Cie.
Paris

Registered Bébé Tentation as a trademark in 1900.

Alexandre Nicholas Théroude
Paris

An early automaton maker, Théroude produced both walking and talking dolls, as well as ordinary kid-bodied dolls, from 1842 until 1895.

Francis Thieck and Jean Born & Cie.
Paris

Registered Seraphin as a trademark, 1923.

SERAPHIN

Thomas R. Thompson
New Haven, Connecticut

Registered his trademark in 1919 for wooden dolls.

Madamoiselle Valentine Thomson
Paris

Registered the trademark Pandore for dolls in 1915.

PANDORE

A. Thuillier
Paris

Made bébés and dolly-faced dolls on jointed wooden, kid, or composition bodies, 1875-1890. The AT marks shown have been attributed to Thuillier.

$$A8T$$

$$AT \cdot N^{\circ}8$$

Thüringer Puppen-Industrie
Waltershausen, Germany

Registered T.P.I., T.P.I.W. and Pola as trademarks for rubber dolls and jointed dolls in 1923.

Thüringer Puppen- und Spielwaren Export
Berlin

Registered the trademarks **Primula** (1923) and **Lopto** (1924).

Thüringer Stoffpuppen-Fabrik
Bad Berka, Germany

Registered **Weimarpuppen**//**Weimarpuppchen** as a trademark for its cloth dolls in 1923.

Tip Top Toy Co.
New York City

Founded in 1912, this manufacturer made composition dolls, including novelties such as **Kewpies** intended for use as carnival prizes (under license from Borgfeldt) and imported bisque heads from German firms such as Kämmer & Reinhardt and Franz Schmidt. Among the dolls it advertised were:

Atlantic City Belle (1919)
Bertie (1913)
Cherry Blossom (1919)
Cy from Siwash (1913)
Dottie Dimples (1913)
Georgiette (1919)
Gertie (1913)
Jim Thorpe (1913)
Little Boy Blue (1913)
Little Johnny Jones (1913)
Little Miss Sunshine (1913)
Maiden America (1918)
Miss Firefly (1913)

Miss Summertime (1919)
Mistress Mary (1913)
Paul (1912)
Prize Baby (1919)
Pudgie (1919)
Shimmy Dolls (1921)
Tip Top Baby (1919)
Tommie Jones (1913)
Virginia (1912)

Of these only **Paul** and **Virginia**—and possibly **Tip Top Baby**—are known to have been made by Tip Top Toy Co. The others were distributed by the firm.

Tourrel
(see Henri Alexandre and Jules Steiner)

The Toy Shop
New York City

Founded in 1922. Made dolls, including **Aunt Jemima** (1923), **Jack & Jill** (1925), **Pickaninny Baby** (1925), and **U-Man Doll** (1923). Used the entwined **TS** initials shown as a mark.

Carl Trautmann
Finsterbergen, Germany

Founded in 1884, Carl Trautmann manufactured ball-jointed dolls, using bisque heads from Simon & Halbig exclusively. The firm was moved to Catterfeld in 1906, at which time it became Catterfelder Puppenfabrik, which see.

**S & H
C.T.
7**

Trego Doll Manufacturing Co.
New York City

Made dolls, 1918-1921. Registered its trademark for ball-jointed dolls with bisque heads in 1919; trademark was used on a label affixed to the doll.

Trion Toy Co.
Brooklyn

Made dolls, 1915-1921. Most named dolls introduced in its first year were designed by Ernesto Peruggi. Among the trade names introduced were:

Cheery (1916)
Chubby (1915)
Georgy-Porgy (1915)
Happy (1915)
Limber Lou (1921)
Little Rascal (1915)
My Belle Marianne (1919)
Pa-na-ma (1915—designed by Adolph Cohen)

Pettish Polly (1915)
Sanitrion (1916)
Smiles (1915)
Sunshine (1915)
Toodles (1915)

Madame Triquet
Rouen, France

Sold and repaired dolls, c. 1900. Mark shown appeared on bodies.

Tut Manufacturing Co.
Los Angeles

Registered its trademark for dolls in 1923.

U

Henry Ulhenhuth & Cie.
Paris

Made kid, bisque, and composition dolls, 1876-1890. Used the trade name **Bébé Merveilleux** for *bébés incassables,* 1890.

Sigmund Ullmann
Sonneberg and Nuremberg,
Germany

Doll exporter, 1922-1926. Registered two
SUN trademarks, 1926.

Uneeda Doll Co.
New York City

Established in 1917, this American
manufacturer first made washable cloth
dolls, and later added composition and
vinyl to its repertoire. It is still in business
today. Early examples of its products were
sometimes marked UNEEDA DOLL or
UNEEDA on the heads. In 1923, Uneeda
advertised a line of rag dolls called Cra-
Doll, which had been introduced by Doll
Craft Company a year earlier. In 1924, it
advertised a doll called Baby Betty.

Unger, Schneider and Hutschen-
reuther
(see Carl Schneider, Erben)

United Porcelain Factory of
Köppelsdorf
(see Ernst Heubach)

United States Rubber Co.
(see Mechanical Rubber Co.)

Utley Co.
Holyoke, Massachusetts

Founded in 1916, Utley made cloth and
papier-mâché dolls, sold under the trade
names Fabco (1917) and Tuco (1918). After
1917, some of the firm's doll bodies were
stamped with the trademark Sanigenic.
Utley dolls most prized by collectors are
those designed by Gertrude Rollinson
(1916); the cloth dolls display a diamond-
shaped stamp on the front of the torso,
within which are the words Rollin-
son//Doll//Holyoke Mass. surrounding a
picture of a doll. Utley's dolls were distributed by Strobel & Wilkin and Louis
Wolf.

V

Verdier & Gutmacher
Paris

Made unbreakable dolls and dolls' heads
of specially treated cloth, 1897-1902.
Known as Verdier & Cie after 1899, al-

though the company used the initials V.G.
and registered four trademarks, also in
1899, which included the initials following:

BÉBÉ EXCELSIOR V.G.

BÉBÉ LE SELECT.V.G.
BÉBÉ MÉTROPOLE.V.G.
BÉBÉ MONOPOLE.V.G.

Gabrielle Verita
Paris

Registered her trademark for rag dolls in 1915.

J. Verlingue
Boulogne-sur-Mer and Montreuil-sous-Bois, France

Made bisque dolls' heads and bathing dolls, 1915-1921; used the initials JV and an **anchor** as part of the mark. Dolls attributed to Verlingue include two marked **Liane** and **Lutin.**

LUTIN
FRANCE

Verry Fils
Paris

Dealt in bisque-headed lady dolls with kid bodies, 1865-1873. Mark shown appeared on the body.

Jeanne Violon
La Varenne-Saint-Hilaire, France

Registered **Jeannine** as a trademark for dolls, 1924.

JEANNINE

Alfred Vischer & Co.
New York City

Importer and agent for Buschow & Beck, 1894-1905. Registered **Minerva** (metal head made by Buschow & Beck) as a trademark, 1901.

Guglielmo Voccia
New York City

Registered several copyrights for dolls, 1919-1920, including **Bella Veneziana, Clown, I Love You, Keep Kool, Lily Tiso, Oriental, Sentimentale,** and **Shy Girl.**

Voices, Inc.
(see Art Metal Works)

Friedrich Voigt
Sonneberg, Germany

Founded in 1879, the firm produced wood, celluloid, and bisque dolls' heads and jointed dolls after c. 1904; used the

trademark **Frivona.** The company was in business until the 1930s.

Roger Vormus
Paris

Registered **Kissmy** as a trademark for dolls, 1920.

W

Wagner & Zetsche
Ilmenau, Germany

Wagner & Zetsche made dolls' bodies of cloth, leather, papier mâché, and imitation leather from 1875 until 1929. The factory sold dolls with heads by Gebrüder Heubach until about 1916, when it acquired, from P. R. Zierow of Berlin, the patent for a composition material and process called **Haralit.** Its character dolls **Harald** (1915), **Inge** (1916), and **Hansi** (1925) thenceforth had Haralit heads. Wagner & Zetsche's elaborate **WZ** trademark has been found on dolls' heads; the signature, **Wag Wag,** was used on the sole of a doll's foot. The **1875** mark appeared on labels, while the **W.Z.** marks of its character dolls, including those with heads made by Heubach, were etched on the backs of the heads.

Izannah F. Walker
Central Falls, Rhode Island

Mrs. Walker patented her rag doll in 1873, though she had probably been making them for a number of years. The dolls, of stockinet stuffed with cotton or hair, sometimes had the patent date marked on their heads.

Patented Nov. 4th 1873

Waltershäuser Puppenfabrik
Waltershausen, Germany

Made dolls' bodies, doll parts, and accessories, 1921-c. 1925. Registered the trademarks **WP** (1921), **Primrose** (1922), and **Walpu** (1925). WP has been found stamped on dolls' bodies.

Johann Walther
Öslau, Germany

Founded in 1900, made dolls' heads c. 1908. In that same year, Johann Walther founded the porcelain factory which later became known as Walther & Sohn (see following listing). His **IW** mark, shown here, was transferred to his new enterprise.

GERMANY
80
11/0

J. Walther & Sohn
Öslau, Germany

This porcelain factory was founded in 1908 by Johann Walther; it produced bisque heads, bathing dolls, and all-bisque dolls

until the 1940s. The firm's entwined **WS** mark was erroneously attributed to Strobel & Wilkin until properly identified by Jürgen & Marianne Cieslik. The mark, with and without the **crown**, was used by Walther & Sohn after 1921. Prior to that year, the firm was known as Walther & Company and most likely used Walther's original IW mark, shown in the previous listing.

The Wazu Novelty Co.
New York City

Registered its trademark in 1922 for dolls and mannequins.

William Augustus Webber
Medford, Massachusetts

Webber developed a very popular singing doll which was operated by a series of reeds. Between 1882 and 1884, the doll sold by the thousands and could be ordered with a choice of more than twenty different songs. Webber dolls had German or French wax-over-composition heads and kid bodies. The bodies were stamped on the lower back as shown here, in addition to the various patent dates and countries in which the patents were registered between 1881 and 1882. A button on the stomach was pushed to make the doll sing.

Weidemann Co.
New York City

Served as an agent for European and American doll makers and importers, 1922-1923.

Weiskirchlitzer Steingutfabrik
Weiskirchlitz, Bohemia

Founded in 1817; made dolls' heads c. 1920. Note the similarity of its mark to that of Walther & Sohn and to the trademark of Strobel & Wilken.

Heinrich Weiss
Sonneberg, Germany

Registered a trademark in 1895 for dressed and undressed dolls.

Weiss, Kühnert & Co.
Gräfenthal, Germany

Founded c. 1891, this porcelain factory made bathing dolls, and later tea-cozy dolls, from about 1910 to at least 1930.

4703

Weiss Kühnert
&
Co
Gräfenthal.
5
Made in
Germany,

Welsch & Co.
Sonneberg, Germany

Founded in 1911, this doll factory used dolls' heads from Max Oscar Arnold for about six years. After 1917, the company purchased heads from Schützmeister & Quendt and Simon & Halbig.

150
Made in Germany
Welsch
9/0

SIMON & HALBIG

WELSCH

F. Welsch
Breslau, Germany

Founded in 1907, this doll factory produced dolls' accessories and doll clothes; after 1922 novelty dolls and miniatures were added to its repertoire. Its **Rose-Puppe** trademark was registered in 1925 for stuffed dolls and dolls' house dolls. The **F.W.B.** mark was incised on an all-bisque doll.

F.W.
B.
GERMANY

Theodor Wendt
Hamburg, Germany

Export firm; registered its **TW** trademark in 1924.

Paul Wernicke
Waltershausen, Germany

Paul Wernicke left the firm of König & Wernicke in 1924 and established a new doll factory. He registered his **Wernicke Puppe** trademark in 1925, and advertised dolls and babies for several years thereafter.

Willi Weyh
Sonneberg, Germany

The Weyh factory and export company operated c. 1924-1925. The mark shown is incised on a bisque character head.

Germany
W. Weyh
4

Hugo Wiegand
Waltershausen, Germany

Founded in 1911, this doll factory produced

character dolls and bent-limb babies. It registered several trademarks for dolls, including **Edelkind** (1918), **Herzlieb** (1913), **Sonny Boy** (1930), and **Sweet Nell** (1925). The mark shown with mold number 1351 was made for the Wiegand company by Simon & Halbig.

$$
\begin{array}{ll}
\text{H.W.} & \text{Germany} \\
\text{W.} & \text{133} \\
\text{1351} & \text{H 3 W} \\
\text{40} &
\end{array}
$$

Wiesenthal, Schindel & Kallenberg
Waltershausen, Germany

Founded in 1858 as Titus Schindel & Company, this factory made papier-mâché figures and costumed dolls. It was known as Wiesenthal, Schindel & Kallenberg by 1893, after which it began to produce jointed dolls with bisque or wax heads, including bent-limb babies and character dolls as the 20th century progressed. The company was in business until c. 1926. Many of its bisque heads were made by Simon & Halbig, as the marks indicate; heads with mold numbers 130 and 150 were made by Hertel, Schwab & Company. Among other known mold numbers are 541 and 1321.

$$
\textit{SIMON & HALBIG} \\
\textit{WSK 4½} \\
\text{WSK} \\
\text{541} \\
\text{4}
$$

Wilhelmsfeld
(see F & W Goebel)

Ernst Winkler
Sonneberg, Germany

Established in 1903, Winkler produced dressed dolls and dolls' heads. Its **Gekleidete Puppe** (dressed doll) trademark was registered in 1910, **Winkler Puppe** and the initials **EW** within a **seven-pointed star** in 1925. All three were used on packaging only. A simple **W** was incised on doll heads. The firm went bankrupt in 1927.

$$
\begin{array}{c}
\text{1910} \\
\text{W.} \\
\text{11/ox}
\end{array}
$$

Friedrich Edmund Winkler
Sonneberg, Germany

Registered **Bébé Articulé** and **FEW** as trademarks for jointed dolls, 1899. Made ball-jointed dolls with bisque heads and character dolls until c. 1912.

Adolf Wislizenus
Waltershausen, Germany

Founded in 1851, this Waltershausen factory was taken over by Adolf Wislizenus c. 1870 and thereafter had several other owners. The company made wax heads during the late 1870s and early '80s; after 1894 it produced some ingeniously jointed doll bodies as well. Its **Old Glory** trademark, registered in 1902, was intended for jointed dolls; these generally had heads by Simon & Halbig, from whom Wislizenus ordered several different mold numbers (1249 and the popular 1079 have been documented). The company also used Bähr & Pröschild molds 252 and 289, but after 1910 ordered heads exclusively from Ernst Heubach. Of the marks shown, most were incised on heads; the one which includes **AWW//DRGM** and a number was used as a body stamp. The trademark **Queen Quality** was registered in 1910; **Mein Glückskind** (My Lucky Child) and **Spezial Serie**, in 1919.

AW
W
DRGM
421481

Heubach-Köppelsdorf
A.W.
W
Germany
9

Gustav Wohlleben
Neustadt, Germany

Founded in 1909; manufactured a variety of dolls and dolls' heads until at least 1936. The mark shown was incised on bodies.

Otto Wohlmann
Nuremberg, Germany

Founded in 1908; manufactured cloth dolls and character dolls. The **OWN** trademark was registered in 1913.

Hermann Wolf
Nordhausen, Germany

Made all-bisque dolls, c. 1922-1930. The firm's **wolf** trademark was registered in 1923. The letters **E.N.SP.F.** following Hermann Wolf's initials (he was presumably the founder) stand for Erste Nordhäuser Spielwarenfabrik—the First Nordhausen

Toy Factory—the name by which the company was known.

Louis Wolf & Co.
Sonneberg, Germany; Boston; and New York City

Founded c. 1870, the Wolf firm distributed both German and American dolls. In addition, Wolf commissioned special designs from a number of companies, including C. M. Bergmann; Hertel, Schwab; and Armand Marseille. Molds 152 (**Our Baby**), 200 (a character doll), and 222 (**Our Fairy**) were ordered from Hertel, Schwab. Many heads were ordered from Armand Marseille (those marked with the **anchor** and **W** were made after 1896). Bisque-headed dolls handled exclusively by Wolf after 1916 sometimes carry the initials **L.W. & Co.** in addition to size and mold number. Among the trade names Wolf handled were:

Baby Belle (1914)
Baby Irene (1913)
Baby Sunshine (1925)
Chubby (1914)
Cinderella (1892)
Columbia (1904)
Excelsior (1911—see mark)
Featherweight (1906)
Grunty Grunts and Smiley Smiles (1921)
Happiness Dolls (1925)
Kutie Kid (1919)
Little Jimmy (1913)
Mangolin (1907)
Mickey (1920)
Minerva (1906)
My Companion (1910)
Our Fairy (1914—see mark: used as sticker)
Playtime (1906)
Pretty Peggy (1925)
Queen Louise (1910)
Rollinson (1916)
Schilling (1910)
Superba (1904)

152
L.W.& Cº
12

Wolf Doll Co., Inc.
New York City

Registered its **Hans Brinker** trademark in 1922 and its **wolf** trademark in 1926. Used the trade name **Two-In-One-Doll** (1922).

Mary Francis Woods
Portland, Oregon

Designed and made composition dolls from 1904 to c. 1925. The dolls portrayed Indian characters whose names included **Chief Joseph** (1904), **Chief Wolf Robe** (1915), **Cigarette Friend** (1915), **Old Angeline** (1915), **Princess Angeline** (1905), and **Sacajewa** (1915). All were distributed exclusively by Konstructo Company of New York City.

H. Wordtmann
Hamburg, Germany

Registered **Puspi** as a trademark for dolls, 1925.

Württembergische Spielwaren-fabrik
Mergelstetten, Germany

Registered **Heidekopf Spielwaren** trademark in 1924 for toys and dolls.

Z

P. R. Zast
Poland

Made celluloid dolls with cloth bodies during the 1920s. The mark shown was used on the shoulder; the initials **A.S.K.** within a **triangle** appeared on the head.

Zeuch & Lausmann
Sonneberg, Germany

Founded in 1888, Zeuch & Lausmann made dolls' heads, dressed dolls, jointed dolls, and musical dolls c. 1894-1925. Its trademark was registered in 1895.

Paul Lucien Zierl
Coeuilly-Champigny-sur-Marne, France

Registered **Le Joujou Pneu** as a trademark for rubber dolls in 1925.

LE JOUJOU PNEU

P. R. Zierow
Berlin

Founded in 1882, this factory originally made wax dolls. After 1905, it produced dolls' bodies with celluloid parts. The **PZ** trademark was registered in 1910; **Mein Augenstern** (Star in my eye) in 1914.

Gottlieb Zinner & Söhne
Schalkau, Germany

Founded in 1845, Zinner specialized in automata and novelties. It also produced dressed dolls and jointed dolls between 1921 and 1935.

Emil Zitsmann
Steinach, Germany

Founded in 1888; made leather, cloth, and imitation leather dolls' bodies and parts until c. 1930. Registered its **anchor** trademark in 1913.

BIBLIOGRAPHY

Anderton, Johana Gast. *More Twentieth Century Dolls: From Bisque to Vinyl.* Rev. ed. 2 vols. Des Moines: Wallace-Homestead Book Co., 1974.

Angione, Genevieve. *All-Bisque and Half-Bisque Dolls.* Camden, N.J.: Thomas Nelson & Sons, 1969.

Bach, Jean. *Collecting German Dolls.* Secaucus, N.J.: Lyle Stuart, Inc., 1983.

_____. *The Main Street Pocket Guide to Dolls.* Pittstown, N.J.: The Main Street Press, 1983.

Buchholz, Shirley. *A Century of Celluloid Dolls.* Cumberland, Md.: Hobby House Press, 1983.

Christopher, Catherine. *The Complete Book of Doll Making and Collecting.* New York: Greystone Press, 1949.

Cieslik, Jürgen and Marianne. *Dolls.* London: Studio Vista/Christie's, 1979.

_____. *German Doll Encyclopedia 1800-1939.* Cumberland, Md.: Hobby House Press, 1985.

Coleman, Elizabeth A. *Dolls, Makers and Marks.* Washington, D.C.: Dorothy S. Coleman, 1966.

Coleman, Evelyn, Elizabeth, and Dorothy. *The Age of Dolls.* Washington, D.C.: Dorothy S. Coleman, 1965.

_____. *The Collector's Encyclopedia of Dolls.* New York: Crown Publishers, 1968.

Fawcett, Clara Hallard. *Dolls: A New Guide for Collectors.* Boston: Charles T. Branford Co., 1964.

Foley, Daniel. *Toys Through the Ages.* Philadelphia: Chilton Books, 1962.

Foulke, Jan. *Blue Book Dolls & Values* (series). Cumberland, Md.: Hobby House Press, 1974-84.

_____. *Focusing On . . . Gebruder Heubach Dolls.* Cumberland, Md.: Hobby House Press, 1980.

_____. *Focusing On . . . Treasury of Mme. Alexander Dolls.* 2nd ed. Cumberland, Md.: Hobby House Press, 1983.

_____. *Kestner: King of Dollmakers.* Cumberland, Md.: Hobby House Press, 1982.

_____. *Simon & Halbig Dolls: The Artful Aspect.* Cumberland, Md.: Hobby House Press, 1984.

Fraser, Antonia. *Dolls.* New York: G. P. Putnam's Sons, 1963.

Freeman, Ruth and Larry. *Cavalcade of Toys.* New York: Century House, 1942.

Gordon, Lesley. *A Pageant of Dolls.* New York: A. A. Wyn, Inc., 1949.

_____. *Peepshow into Paradise.* New York: John de Graff, Inc., 1953.

Hillier, Mary. *Dolls and Doll Makers.* New York: G. P. Putnam's Sons, 1968.

Jacobs, Flora Gill and Estrid Faurholt. *A Book of Dolls & Doll Houses.* Rutland, Vt.: Charles E. Tuttle Co., 1967.

King, Constance Eileen. *The Collector's History of Dolls.* New York: St. Martin's Press, 1978.

_____. *Jumeau: Prince of Dollmakers.* Cumberland, Md.: Hobby House Press, 1983.

Lavitt, Wendy. *Dolls.* The Knopf Collectors' Guides to American Antiques. New York: Alfred A. Knopf, 1983.

Merrill, Madeline Osborne. *The Art of Dolls 1700-1940.* Cumberland, Md.: Hobby House Press, 1985.

Manos, Susan. *Schoenhut Dolls & Toys.* Paducah, Ky.: Collector Books, 1976.

Noble, John. *Dolls.* New York: Walker and Company, 1967.

Richter, Lydia. *The Beloved Käthe-Kruse-Dolls: Yesterday and Today.* Cumberland, Md.: Hobby House Press, 1983.

St. George, Eleanor. *Dolls of Three Centuries.* New York: Charles Scribner's Sons, 1951.

Schoonmaker, Patricia N. *Effanbee Dolls.* Cumberland, Md.: Hobby House Press, 1984.

_____. *Research on Kämmer & Reinhardt Dolls.* 1965.

INDEX OF DESIGNERS

INDEX OF MARKS

I. Numerals

265,	10, 69	326,	86	373,	73
266,	60, 86	327,	18, 86	374,	10
267,	60	328,	86	375,	10, 86, 94
268,	60	329,	86	376,	10, 86
269,	10, 60, 112	330,	10, 49	377,	73, 86
270,	10, 26, 71, 86	332,	119	378,	10, 86
271,	60	333,	86, 119	379,	10
272,	71	334,	60, 119	380,	10, 83
273,	10, 86	335,	119	381,	10
274,	60	336,	119	382,	86
275,	10, 60, 86	337,	119	384,	86
276,	60, 74, 86	338,	119	389,	10
277,	10	339,	60, 119	390,	10, 86, 92, 94, 100
278,	10	340,	10, 49, 60, 119	390a,	86
279,	71	341,	60, 86, 87, 119	391,	86, 94
281,	10, 60, 71	341k,	86	393,	10
282,	60, 71, 72	341ka,	86	394,	10
283,	10, 49, 60	342,	10, 60, 86, 119	395,	86, 125
284,	60	343,	10-11, 60, 119	396,	83, 86
285,	10, 49, 73	344,	60, 119	398,	86
286,	49	345,	60, 86	399,	60, 83, 86
287,	10	348,	10, 60		
289,	10, 60, 140	349,	60	400,	60, 69, 86
291,	60	350,	10, 49, 60, 86	401,	69, 86, 125
292,	10, 60, 71, 72, 73	351,	83, 86, 119	402,	69
293,	73, 112	351k,	86	403,	69
297,	10	352,	86, 119	406,	60, 69, 86
299,	73	353,	83, 86, 119	407,	60
		354,	119	410,	84
300,	10, 60, 86, 116	355,	119	411,	86
301,	16, 41, 60, 116, 121	356,	86, 119	414,	5, 60, 86
302,	10, 60	357,	119	415,	119
303,	73	358,	119	416,	119
305,	10, 73, 119	359,	119	417,	119
306,	10	360,	119	418,	60, 119
309,	10, 86	360a,	86	419,	119
310,	86	361,	119	420,	55, 119
312,	60, 117	362,	83, 86, 119	421,	119
313,	10, 60	363,	119	422,	119
317,	49, 60	364,	119	423,	119
318,	86	365,	119	424,	10, 119
319,	49	366,	119	425,	10, 119
320,	10, 49, 60, 86	367,	119	426,	119
321,	10, 49, 60	368,	119	427,	60, 119
322,	10, 49, 86	369,	86, 119	428,	119
323,	10, 60, 86	370,	73, 86, 94, 119	429,	119
324,	10, 86	371,	86	430,	119
325,	10, 86	372,	73, 86	431,	119

432,	119	525,	10, 71, 72	567,	71, 72
433,	119	526,	10, 69, 71, 72	568,	10, 71
434,	119	527,	71	570,	71, 85, 119
435,	119	528a,	71	571,	10, 71, 72
437,	60	529,	10, 111	572,	71
438,	60	530,	119	573,	71
439,	60	531,	10, 69, 71, 72	574,	71
441,	10	532,	71, 73	575,	71
444,	60, 83	533,	71	577,	71
445,	60	533a,	71	579,	71
448,	60	534,	71	581,	10
449,	86	535,	10	584,	10
450,	14, 60, 86	535b,	71	585,	10-11
451,	60, 86	536,	10	586,	71
452,	60, 86	537,	71	588,	71
452H,	86	537/2 033,	10	589,	71
454,	86	538,	71	590,	71, 85
458,	60, 86	539,	71	599,	85
459,	60	539/2 023,	10		
463,	60	540,	71, 85, 119	600,	10, 69, 85, 119
471,	60	540-4,	39	601,	71
480,	60	541,	10, 71, 139	604,	10
482,	10	542,	71, 85	607,	119
499,	10	543,	71	608,	71
		544,	71	610,	119
500,	10, 13, 69, 71, 72,	545,	71	611,	119
	73, 85, 114, 119	546,	10, 71, 72	615,	14, 69
501,	49	547,	71	616,	119
501-10,	73	548,	71	619,	10
502,	71	549,	10, 71, 72	620,	85, 119
503,	73	550,	48,69,71,85,119	621,	85
504,	71, 85	550A,	85	624,	10
505,	71, 85	551,	71, 85	626,	69
509,	69	551k,	85	630,	85
510,	41, 69, 85	552,	69	631,	69
511,	69, 71	553,	71	639	2
512,	71	554,	10, 71, 72	640,	10
513,	85	555,	71, 74	640a,	86
514,	57, 71	556,	71	641,	10
515,	85	557,	10, 71	642,	10
516,	71, 85, 119	559,	71	643,	10
517,	71	560,	71, 85	644,	10
518,	71, 85	560A,	85	645,	10
519,	71, 85	560a,	87, 100	646,	10
520,	10, 71, 72, 85	561,	71	651,	69
522,	71	563,	71	652,	69
523,	71	565,	71	665,	69
524,	71	566,	71	670,	86

675,	69
678,	10
680,	72
693,	119
696,	2, 86
698,	2
700,	22, 69, 86
701,	69, 74, 86
707,	10
710,	86
711,	86
715,	69
716,	69
717,	69
718,	69
719,	69, 119
720,	69, 119
721,	69
726,	69
727,	69
728,	69, 119
729,	119
730,	69
738,	119
739,	119
740,	119
748,	119
749,	119
750,	86, 119
758,	119
759,	119
760,	86
768,	119
769,	119
772,	2
773,	69
775,	69
776,	69
777,	69, 74
778,	119
784,	2
790,	86
799,	10
800,	69, 86, 101
810,	86
817,	69

820,	86
826,	69
828,	69, 101
830,	101
831,	69
837,	119
845,	119
846,	119
847,	119
848,	119
852,	119
866,	2
867,	2
868,	2
869,	2
870,	2
873,	69
878,	119
880,	2, 119
881,	119
886,	119
886.2,	5
887,	119
890,	2, 88, 119
894,	2
896,	119
898,	119
899,	119
900,	69, 73, 86, 114
901,	69
904,	101
905,	119
908,	119
909,	119
914,	101, 114
916,	101
917,	69
918,	119
919,	119
920,	86, 119
921,	69, 119
924,	101
926,	69, 101
927	86, 101, 112, 119
928,	101
929,	101, 119
939,	119

940,	119
941,	119
949,	119
950,	86, 101, 119
951,	86
952,	69
959,	119
966,	86
968,	119
969,	107, 119
970,	86, 119
971,	86
971a,	86
972,	86
973,	69, 86
974,	2
975,	46, 69, 86
977,	69
979,	2, 119
980,	86
984,	86
985,	86
989,	119
990,	86
991,	86
992,	86
993,	86
995,	86
996,	86
997,	86
1000,	2, 119, 125
1005/3652,	10
1008,	2, 119
1009,	119
1010,	119
1018,	119
1019,	119
1020,	2, 93
1024,	3
1026,	3
1028,	3
1029,	119
1038,	119
1039,	119
1040,	119
1041,	119
1044,	3

1046,	3, 105	1231,	86	1322,	3
1049,	119	1234,	3	1326,	3
1056,	3	1235,	3	1329,	119
1058,	119	1236,	3	1330,	86
1059,	119	1237,	3	1335,	86
1060,	119	1246,	119	1339,	82
1061,	119	1248,	119	1340,	119
1062,	3	1249,	53, 119, 140	1342,	3
1064,	3	1250,	3, 112, 119	1346,	3
1068,	119	1253,	112	1348,	36-37
1069,	119	1254,	3	1349,	36-37
1078,	119	1259,	112	1351,	139
1079,	93, 119, 140	1260,	3, 119	1352,	3
1080,	119	1261,	3	1353,	2
1081,	119	1262,	112	1357,	3, 26
1086,	3	1263,	112	1358,	3, 119
1092,	3	1266,	112	1360,	3
1098,	119	1267,	112	1361,	3
1099,	119	1268,	3	1362,	3
1100,	25-26	1269,	3, 119	1366,	3
1108,	119	1270,	3, 112	1367,	3
1109,	119	1271,	3, 112	1368,	3, 119
1121,	3	1272,	112	1369,	86
1123,	3	1274,	112	1370,	86, 119
1129,	119	1278,	119	1373,	3
1139,	119	1279,	3, 119	1374,	86
1142,	3	1280,	119	1376,	3, 116
1148,	119	1288,	3	1388,	119
1150,	119	1289,	119	1394,	24
1152,	3	1290,	3	1397,	119
1153,	3	1291,	3	1398,	119
1158,	119	1293,	112	1400,	114
1159,	119	1294,	119	1400/4,	25
1160,	119	1295,	112	1402,	3
1170,	3, 119	1296,	112	1409,	112
1171,	3	1297,	112	1426,	119
1172,	3	1298,	112	1428,	119
1173,	3	1299,	112	1429,	53, 97, 140
1174,	3	1300,	119	1430,	97
1175,	3	1301,	119	1432,	3
1176,	3	1302,	119	1440,	97
1177,	3	1303,	119	1448,	119
1180,	112, 119	1304,	119	1465,	119
1199,	119	1305,	119	1468,	36
1200,	26	1307,	119	1469,	36-37
1210,	3	1308,	119	1478,	119
1222,	3	1310,	112	1485,	119
1226,	3	1321,	3, 139		

1488,	119	2096,	111	6894,	60
1489,	119	2097,	111	6896,	60
1496,	119	2098,	111	6897,	60
1498,	119	2154,	111	6969,	60
1527,	119	2500,	114	6970,	60
1616,	119	2736,	36	6971,	60
1748,	119	2780,	81		
1776,	36			7027,	60
1800,	114	3000,	85	7064,	60
1848,	36	3091,	85	7072,	60
1849,	36	3093,	85	7077,	60
1893,	36	3200,	85	7106,	60
1894,	100	3333,	86	7109,	60
1896,	36	3500,	85	7124,	60
1898,	36	3600,	85	7129,	60
1899,	103	3700,	85	7134,	60
1900,	114			7139,	60
1901.2,	111	4000,	114	7226,	60
1904,	41, 114	4001,	114	7246,	60
1905,	41	4008,	85	7247,	60
1906,	41, 114	4500,	114	7248,	60
1909,	105, 114	4515,	93	7256,	60
1910,	139	4600,	114	7306,	60
1912,	36	4700,	114	7314,	60
1914,	36	4703,	137	7326,	60
1916,	119	4900,	114	7345,	60
1920,	36, 89			7346,	60
1922,	36-37			7402,	60
1930,	72, 114-15	5000,	114	7407,	60
		5050,	104	7550,	60
		5300,	114	7602,	60
2000,	85, 95	5500,	114	7603,	60
2010,	85, 95	5625,	60	7604,	60
2015,	85	5636,	60	7614,	60
2020,	93	5689,	60	7620,	60
2023,	111	5700,	114	7622,	60
2025,	111	5773,	60	7623,	60
2048,	111	5777,	54, 60	7624,	60
2068,	111	5800,	114	7625,	60
2070,	111			7631,	60
2074,	111	6335,	81	7634,	60
2075,	111	6688,	60	7635,	60
2081,	111	6692,	60	7636,	60
2084,	111	6736,	60, 83	7637,	60
2085,	111	6774,	60	7644,	60
2092,	111	6789,	136	7650,	60
2094,	111	6891,	60	7657,	60
2095,	111	6892,	60	7658,	60

7659,	60	7971,	60	8822,	81
7669,	60	7975,	60	8867,	81
7670,	60	7977,	60	8878,	60
7671,	60				
7679,	60	8017,	60	9027,	81
7686,	60	8050,	60	9042,	60
7687,	60	8055,	60	9056,	60
7692,	60	8191,	60	9081,	60
7701,	60	8192,	60	9085,	60
7703,	60	8195,	60	9141,	60
7711,	60	8226,	60	9167,	60
7714,	60	8306,	60	9209,	60
7739,	60	8309,	60	9219,	60
7740,	60	8413,	60	9307,	81
7743,	60	8416,	60	9355,	60
7744,	60	8420,	60	9457,	60
7745,	60	8457,	60	9500,	57
7759,	60	8459,	60	9513,	60
7760,	60	8473,	60	9572,	60
7761,	60	8547,	60	9578,	60
7763,	60	8548,	60	9594,	60
7764,	60	8552,	81		
7768,	60	8553,	81	10000	81
7788,	60	8572,	60	10532,	60
7843,	60	8588,	60	10539,	60
7850,	60	8589,	60	10556,	60
7851,	60	8606,	60	10557,	60
7864,	60	8660,	81	10586,	60
7867,	60	8675,	81	10588,	60
7869,	60	8682,	81	10617,	60
7885,	60	8724,	60	10633,	60
7890,	60	8729,	60	10727,	60, 96
7911,	60	8764,	60	10731,	60
7925,	60	8774,	60	10790,	60
7926,	60	8778,	60	11010,	60, 96
7956,	60	8801,	60	12386,	60

II. Dates

1772,	81	1895,	85, 107
1827,	28	1896,	85
1844-1847,	75	1897,	85
1849-1870,	75	1898,	85
May 6, 1851,	50	1899,	85
1852//75 1927,	43	1900,	60, 85, 114
29 APRIL//1857,	92	Feb 13, 1900,	8
March 30th, '58,	51	1901,	85, 111
[18]60,	82	July 8th 1901,	22
1865,	50	1902,	85
May 1st 1866,	31	1903,	85, 103
1867,	64	1904,	1, 101
March 24th, 1868,	66	1905,	85
Sept. 8, 1868,	56	1906,	118
Nov. 4th 1873,	136	1907,	101
MARCH 24th 1874,	77	1909,	85
1875,	135	1910,	63, 139
July 27, 1875,	66	1911,	5
September 21, 1875,	63	JAN. 17TH 1911,	115
1876,	7	NOV. 9, 1912,	120
1878,	67	1913,	101, 115
1879,	135	1914,	5, 80
April 29 '79,	66	Sept. 7, 1915,	51
Dec. 7 '80,	12, 66	1916,	13, 63
1881,	137	1920,	97
1882,	137	1921,	5
Nov. 7 '82,	66	Sept. 8, 1921,	79
1890,	85	1922,	104
1892,	7, 85	1923,	40, 104
1893,	85	1924,	63, 99
Aug. 15th 1893,	28	1930,	72
1894,	85, 86, 100		

III. Letters, Initials, and Abbreviations

A,	78, 79, 102, 126, 129	B.P.D. Co.,	20
AB [entwined],	3, 20	BSW,	111
AB&G,	3	BV,	129
A.B.C.,	3	BW,	15
ABD Co.,	5		
ABG [entwined],	3	C,	43, 102, 115, 126
ACV [entwined],	52	Caho,	24
A.D,	20	C. & S.,	30
Ad'E,	34	CB,	14, 27
AF,	44	CDCO,	26
AF & C,	44	C'Dep.,	37
AH,	55, 57	CE & S,	40
AH//S,	59	CEGD [entwined],	52
AHW,	63-64	CEUS,	40
AL,	78	CF & Co.,	43
AL & Cie,	78	CH,	56
ALBEGO,	2, 3	CHN [entwined],	62
AM,	1, 18, 37, 39, 46, 83, 85-87, 125	CK [entwined],	74
		C.M.B.,	13-14
		CMT [entwined],	91
AM [within triangle],	89	CMU,	45
AM & Co,	1	CO,	41
AMN [entwined],	92	COD,	37
Al,	32	CP,	25, 97
A.P.,	80, 103	CR,	108
AR,	5, 105-106, 107	C.T.,	132
ARI,	107	CV [entwined],	73
A.S,	114, 124-5	CZ,	107
AS//K,	142		
ASS,	114	D,	34, 36, 71, 126
AT,	130	DALABA,	114
AV [entwined],	57	D&DC,	38
A.W.,	140	D&KN,	37
AWW,	140	DEP,	43, 118-19
		DI,	129
		DIP,	129
B,	73	DKF,	35
B&D,	12	DP,	53-54, 100
B&P,	11	D.P. Co.,	35
BB,	11	D.R.G.M.,	85, 105
BI,	80, 107	DRMR,	85
B.K,	120	DV,	129
BL,	68		
B.M.,	91	E.B.,	16
BP,	10-11	EB [entwined],	11

IV. Names and Words

A la Clinique des Poupées, 96
A La Galerie Vivienne, 52
A La Poupée de Nuremberg, 1
A. Steiner-Köppelsdorf, 125
A.T. GUILLARD, 52
A. Théroude, 130
Aceedeecee Doll, 5
ACTOE, 128
A. D. BOUCHET, 20
Ada May, 50
Adelene, 81
Adeline, 90
Adlon, 110
Admiral Dewey, 36
Admiral Dot, 65
Admiral Sampson, 36
Admiration, 103
Admiration Babies, 103
Adtocolite, 62
Agnes, 2, 23
Alabama Indestructible Doll, 120
ALAH, 82
Alexander, 2
Alice [script], 102
Alice-in-Wonderland, 2, 27
Alice Lee, 40
Alida, 124
All Steel Dolls, 88
All Wood Perfection Art Dolls, 115
Alma, 17-18, 86
Aluminia, 128
AMBERG'S//VICTORY//DOLL, 5
Amberg's Walking Doll, 3
Ambisc, 3
AMER. CHAR. DOLL CO., 5
AMERICAN, 109
American Beauty, 116, 128
American Beauty Doll, 5
American Dolls for Americans, 3
American Fashion, 128
American Lady, 90
AMERICAN MADE//TOY COM-
PANY, 6
American Maid, 90, 116
American Rose Bud, 34

The American Standard, 3
Amkid, 3
AMOUR-BÉBÉ, 52
AMUSO, 89
Amy, 2, 41
Anne Shirley, 40
Anneliese, 107
Annette, 62
Anniversary Baby, 3
ANSONNET, 102
Anthony, 124
Aprico, 124
Arabesque, 128
Arctic Boy, 65
Armand Marseille, 83, 86-87
Army Nurse, 62
Arnola, 6
ARNOLD PRINT WORKS, 7
Arnoldia, 6
ARRANBEE, 7
ARRANBEE//DOLL CO., 7
ARRANBEE DOLLS, 7
Art Dolls, 62
ART QUALITY//CAMEO DOLLS, 24
ART QUALITY//CAMEO TOYS, 24
ARTICLE//FRANÇAISE, 42
Artiste, 20
Asador, 11
ASCO, 127
Atlantic City Belle, 131
AU BB ROSE, 120
Au Bébé Rose, 120
AU NAIN BLEU, 8
AU PARADIS DES ENFANTS, 8
Augusta, 106
Aunt Dinah, 109
Aunt Jemima, 131
AUX GALLERIES DE FER, 134
AUX REVES DE L'ENFANCE, 9

B. Ravca [script], 105
BABA, 102
Babbit at Your Service, 89
Babes in the Woods, 13
BABET, 77

160

V. Symbols

Anchor, 6, 16, 77, 78, 79, 86, 89, 134, 142, 143
Angel, 26, 66, 111
Anvil, 112
Arm [of jointed doll], 45
Balloon, 131
Bear, 22, 38, 44, 53, 67, 83, 140; holding doll, 56; with clown and doll, 92; with elephant and monkey, 35; with shield, 128
Beaver, 12
Bee. *See* Insect
Bell, 18, 73
Bird, 30, 37, 55, 83, 116. *See also* Eagle
Building, 59
Caduceus, 37
Camel, 124
Cameo, 24
Cat, 19, 59, 124
Cherries, 7
Child [children], 12, 42, 49, 92, 95, 98, 100, 129; with dolls, 17, 48, 49, 96. *See also* Man, Woman
Chinese. *See* Figure
Circle, 1, 4, 12, 14, 15, 16, 17, 18, 22, 33, 42, 43, 44, 45, 46, 51, 53, 58, 67, 70, 71, 75, 88, 91, 99, 102, 110, 113, 114, 124, 129, 131, 138, 139, 140; with diamond, 107; with scalloped edges, 21, 31, 48, 50, 105, 112; with triangle, 96; within circle, 9, 10, 14, 19, 20, 23, 28, 34, 36, 37, 38, 39, 40, 47, 49, 55, 56, 59, 63, 64, 72, 73, 74, 75, 76, 79, 81, 84, 97, 100, 101, 104, 111, 115, 116, 121, 141; within sunburst, 117, 123
Clover, 3-leaf, 22, 73, 81, 132; 4-leaf, 26, 99, 140
Clown, 8, 36, 57, 123; with bear and doll, 92
Coat of arms, 61, 75, 142
Colonel, 2
Cornucopia, 48
Cradle, 35
Cross, 16, 65

Crossbones, 74
Crown, 25, 26, 49, 57, 70-71, 73, 81, 82, 85, 92, 109, 127, 136
Crystal ball, 71
Daisy. *See* Flower
Deer, 38
Diamond, 7, 21, 39, 48, 52, 53, 64, 65, 90, 91, 93, 94, 125, 133; within circle, 107; within diamond, 107, 122, 133, 140
Dog[s], 32, 35, 117
Doll[s], 11, 34, 38, 44, 57, 61, 79, 92, 94, 108, 128, 131, 136, 138; with bonnet, 64; with cape, 110; with crossed hammers, 112; with crown, 39; with flag, 59, 77, 126; with scythe, 14; within circle, 10, 34, 39, 43, 45, 46, 80, 100, 116, 123; within diamond, 53, 133; within oval, 53, 58, 92, 117; within rectangle, 51, 61, 96, 123, 143; within triangle, 138. *See also* Head of doll
Dragon, 122
Eagle, 6, 7, 75, 138; head of, 99. *See also* Bird
Egyptian, 117
Eiffel Tower, 31
Elephant, 35, 41, 124
Elf. *See* Gnome
Elipse. *See* Oval
Eye, 101, 143
Figure[s], Chinese, 118-19; hanging, 132; stick, 107; with square, 127. *See also* Child, Doll, Man, Woman
Fish, 57, 58
Flag[s], 58, 60, 84; crossed, 19, 102, 134
Flower[s], 19, 41, 51, 55, 87, 129. *See also* Clover
Foot [sole of], 68
Globe, 53, 65, 76, 100; with doll, 50, 94
Gnome, 53, 142
Hammers [crossed], 88, 106, 112, 113
Head of doll, 7, 98, 99, 109, 120, 124;